"This book represents an important advance in de-Westernizing media studies. Janet Steele investigates how Muslim journalists in Indonesia and Malaysia apply their religious principles. Rejecting univocal, monolithic notions of religion, the book introduces us to a rich tapestry of media organizations and practitioners, showing how Islam has inspired a wide range of ideological stances and professional role perceptions. For journalism studies, the book invites a rethink of secular liberalism as the only foundation for journalisms that value independence, truth, and justice."
—**Cherian George**, author of *Hate Spin: The Manufacture of Religious Offense and Its Threat to Democracy*

"Steele has written a readable, insightful book about how journalists in Indonesia and Malaysia define professional identity and practice. The analysis is packed with analytical gems and original data that show how journalistic norms conventionally identified with Western journalism, such as truth and justice, are reinterpreted in the context of Islamic culture. With the keen eye of a historian and the sharpness of a longtime scholar of the region, Steele offers important lessons for those interested in understanding the cultures of professional journalism in a globalized world. The book shakes off stereotypes and invites us to study the complex nexus between religiosity and journalism."
—**Silvio Waisbord**, professor of media and public affairs, George Washington University

MEDIATING ISLAM

COSMOPOLITAN JOURNALISMS
IN MUSLIM SOUTHEAST ASIA

Janet Steele

UNIVERSITY OF WASHINGTON PRESS

Seattle

Mediating Islam is published with the assistance of a grant from the Charles and Jane Keyes Endowment for Books on Southeast Asia, established through the generosity of Charles and Jane Keyes.

This book is also supported by a grant from the Donald R. Ellegood International Publications Endowment.

UNIVERSITY OF WASHINGTON PRESS
www.washington.edu/uwpress

LIBRARY OF CONGRESS CATALOGING-IN-PUBLICATION DATA
Names: Steele, Janet E., author.
Title: Mediating Islam : cosmopolitan journalisms in Muslim Southeast Asia / Janet Steele.
Description: Seattle : University of Washington Press, [2018] | Includes bibliographical
    references and index.
Identifiers: LCCN 2017026660 (print) | LCCN 2017027213 (ebook) |
    ISBN 9780295742977 (ebook) | ISBN 9780295742953 (hardcover : alk. paper) |
    ISBN 9780295742960 (pbk. : alk. paper)
Subjects: LCSH: Islamic press—Southeast Asia. | Religious newspapers and periodicals—
    Southeast Asia. | Journalism—Southeast Asia.
Classification: LCC PN5449.A789 (ebook) | LCC PN5449.A789 S74 2018 (print) |
    DDC 079.59088/297—dc23
LC record available at https://lccn.loc.gov/2017026660

Parts of this book were originally published elsewhere and are used again by permission: the introduction, in "Justice and Journalism: Islam and Journalistic Values in Indonesia and Malaysia," *Journalism: Theory, Practice, and Criticism* 12, no. 5 (2011): 533–49; chapter 2, in "From Fashion to the Hereafter: The Case of *Republika*, a Modern Newspaper Serving the Indonesian Muslim Community," *Media Asia* 40, no. 1 (April 2013): 27–33; parts of chapter 4 in "Ramadan in the Newsroom: *Tempo, Malaysiakini*, and the State," in *Religious Pluralism, State, and Society in Asia* (London: Routledge, 2014), 197–215, and "Trial by the Press: An Examination of Journalism, Islam, and Ethics in Indonesia and Malaysia," *International Journal of Press/Politics* 18 (July 2013): 342–59; parts of the conclusion, in "Journalism and 'the Call to Allah': Teaching Journalism in Indonesia's Islamic Universities and State Institutes," *International Journal of Communication* 6 (2012): 2944–61.

For Beth and Jerry

I went to the West and saw Islam, but no Muslims;
I got back to the East and saw Muslims, but not Islam.

—MUHAMMAD ʿABDUH

CONTENTS

ACKNOWLEDGMENTS

Many people have helped with this book, including several who do not agree with its conclusions. First among these is Fauwaz Abdul Aziz, who has given unstintingly of his time and knowledge since he first commented in 2007 that many things about being a journalist did not jibe with the teachings of Islam. This entire project began with Fauwaz, and for his patience, forbearance, and time away from his own work, I owe him a debt that I can never properly pay. Dhimam Abror similarly answered endless questions since the very early days of this project with both kindness and patience, drawing on his unique experience as the chief editor of four different newspapers to offer a wealth of information about journalism and Islam. I know that he, like Fauwaz, does not agree with all of my conclusions.

Journalists at the five publications I studied were unfailingly generous with their time and willingness to answer questions. Although many of their names appear in the text and notes, there are others whose names do not, and I would like to take this opportunity to thank all of those who welcomed me into their newsrooms with open minds and hearts. I am especially grateful to past and present editors Herry Nurdi and Eman Mulyatman (*Sabili*); Nasihin Masha, Heri Ruslan, Arys Hilman, and Elba Damhuri (*Republika*); Steven Gan, Fathi Aris Omar, and Premesh Chandran (*Malaysiakini*); Ahmad Lutfi Othman and Zulkifli Sulong (*Harakah*); and Arif Zulkifli, Hermien Kleiden, Toriq Hadad, S. Malela Mahargasarie, Goenawan Mohamad, and Bambang Harymurti (*Tempo*).

For friendship, support, and numerous conversations over banana leaf lunches, tea, Ramadan treats, dinners at Kokas, and day trips to Bogor, I am grateful to Zakiah Koya, Hazlan Zakaria, Vicknésan Sampasivam, Zhang Su Li, Allison Xavier, Fauwaz Abdul Aziz, Hamida Camlian Alonto, Yusi Avianto Pareanom, Chodidah Budi Rahardjo, and Eko Budi Rahardjo.

Yusi Avianto Pareanom, Dhimam Abror, Fauwaz Abdul Aziz, and two anonymous reviewers read and commented on the entire manuscript. Joel Kuipers has been generous with advice, encouragement, and insights in many conversations along the way. The Sigur Center for Asian Studies provided substantial summer research grants and opportunities to present portions of this book for useful feedback; the George Washington University School of Media and Public Affairs (SMPA) and SMPA director Frank Sesno provided annual research funding and support. Colleagues in SMPA—especially Matt Hindman, Will Youmans, Steve Livingston, Silvio Waisbord, and Kim Gross—read drafts of various parts of the manuscript and offered encouragement. Yvonne Oh, formerly of the US Embassy in Kuala Lumpur, managed to arrange almost annual speaking engagements that helped subsidize my research in Malaysia. Everyone at the University of Washington Press has been extremely helpful, especially Lorri Hagman, who has been both encouraging and attentive since the very beginning; she offered suggestions that greatly improved the manuscript.

I am grateful for the support of my brother, Bayard, and the memory of my mother and father, from whom I inherited both wanderlust and a love of journalism. My biggest debt of all is to Beth Bowen and Jerry Macdonald. They, better than anyone, know how much I owe them.

My spelling of Indonesian and Malay terms and phrases follows local usage, which in the two countries under consideration is not always the same. When citing a previously published work, I use the spelling that appeared in the original. Arabic words follow Indonesian or Malaysian conventions and are presented without diacritical marks.

MEDIATING ISLAM

INTRODUCTION

What is Islamic journalism?

At *Sabili*, an Indonesian Islamist magazine first established in 1984 as an underground paper, journalists are hired for their ability at *dakwah*, or Islamic propagation. They believe that the solution to the ills of modern society lies in the application of sharia, the law laid down in the Qur'an and Sunnah of the Prophet Mohammad in the seventh century. Hudud, the controversial criminal code of sharia, includes the amputation of the hand of the thief and the stoning of married adulterers. Journalists at *Tempo*, however—an Indonesian news weekly that was founded in 1971, banned by the Soeharto regime in 1994, and brought back to print in 1998—don't talk much about Hudud. Despite the fact that more than 80 percent of *Tempo* journalists are Muslim, they don't see themselves as Islamists or believe in the obligation to work for and live under an Islamic state where sharia rules supreme. Although many of them are pious and see their work as a kind of *ibadah* (worship), the Islam they practice is variously described as "cosmopolitan," "progressive," or even "liberal."

So which of these views of Islamic journalism is wrong? Many in the West have a monolithic understanding of Islam; when we think of Islam and the media, we think of the Middle East, Arab culture, a controlled press, and, at worst, terrorism. Of course these views are not limited only to the West. In 2014, when I agreed to speak about my research at a book festival in Eastern Indonesia, I was startled to see my name on the program listed next to the heading "Media and Terrorism." Similarly, we have a monolithic understanding of journalism, assuming that the way we practice it in the West is common to the rest of the world. Much of the media development industry is based on that assumption, exporting Western news practices to developing countries along with press freedom (LaMay 2007; Simon 2014).

My work suggests that neither of these assumptions is true. Over the past two decades, some of the most interesting attempts at democratic reform have occurred within the Muslim world. Some of these transitions, such as the one in Indonesia, have been exemplary, providing inspiration not only to neighboring countries but also serving as a potential model to the rest of the world. Others, such as the "revolution" in Egypt that began in January 2011, have legacies that are far more ambiguous. What has been the relationship between journalism, Islam, and these challenges to authoritarianism? Is there an Islamic form of journalism and, if so, how is it related to democratic reform?

Existing research on journalism and Islam tends to be subsumed into the broader category of Islam and communication. What anthropologist Robert Hefner (1997a, 18) has called the "near-universal" conviction among twentieth-century social scientists "that religion is, at best, a declining historical force, destined to give way to the twin forces of economic modernization and nation-state formation" has continued to influence the way that religion is understood in relation to the development of a modern press system. The 1950s modernization theorists were especially dismissive of the relationship between religion and communication in modern societies. Sociologist Daniel Lerner (2000 [1958], 120), for example, wrote: "Whether from East or West, modernization poses the same basic challenge—the infusion of 'a rationalist and positivist spirit' against which, scholars seem agreed, 'Islam is absolutely defenseless.'"

Despite Lerner's conviction that a modern society would inevitably be secular, a half century later this is not the case. As the Iranian-American communication theorist Hamid Mowlana (2003, 309) has argued, whereas religion in the West is divorced from secular life, and ethical conduct is left to the conscience of the individual, in Islam "this separation of the religious from the secular sphere did not materialize, and if attempts were made by the late modernizers to do this, the process was never completed." Moreover, what Western academic discourse generally sees as a sharp distinction between religious and secular worldviews has been challenged by scholars who question the assumption that liberal secularism is completely divorced from normative conceptions of religion (Mahmood 2009).

The Islamic revivalism of the late twentieth century has prompted some to argue for an Islamic theory of communication. Mowlana (1993, 12) has suggested that an "Islamic community paradigm" based on revelation rather than information infuses communication in Islamic countries. International communication scholar Gholam Khiabany (2006, 5–7) has cautioned against reductionism and observed that a variety of media are consumed by Muslims in a variety of countries that may or may not be majority Muslim. Although both Indonesia and Malaysia have significant sectors of media devoted to propagating Islamic values, most journalists do not work for overtly Islamic publications in either country. While this book considers the views of self-proclaimed Islamists, it also focuses on journalists who work for publications that are not ordinarily considered "Islamic." And although it rejects the notion of an Islamic theory of journalism, it likewise rejects the "commonsense" view of Western theorists that journalism is a fundamentally secular enterprise.

Recent work by political scientist Jeremy Menchik (2016) sheds light on how journalists in Indonesia and Malaysia who reject the labels "liberal" and "secular" can at the same time promote both tolerance and democracy. Noting that "our understanding of the relationship between religion and the state outside of secular-liberal government is limited," Menchik (2016, 3) explicates the views of Muslim organizations in Indonesia that are tolerant but not secular. What he has demonstrated about the existence of tolerance without liberalism in two of the world's largest Muslim organizations, Nahdlatul Ulama (NU) and Muhammadiyah, has direct parallels with what I have found among pious journalists in both Indonesia and Malaysia who support independent media yet work for publications that cannot in any way be described as either liberal or secular.

Another way of thinking about these journalists is as "cosmopolitans." Cosmopolitanism has been variously characterized as world citizenship, a willingness to engage with others, or a "middle-path alternative . . . between ethnocentric nationalism and particularistic multiculturalism" (Vertovec and Cohen 2002, 1). It can be an alternative to the nation-state or, on a more personal level, "the ability to stand outside of having one's life written and scripted by any one community" (Hall 2002, 26). Within the context of Islam, cosmopolitanism has been manifested in what historian Carool Kersten

(2009) has described as a third alternative for those who seek "to navigate between outright secularism, bland traditionalism, and uncompromisingly literalist reinterpretations of Islamic teaching." In Indonesia it has been most evident in the "new Muslim intelligentsia," scholars and intellectuals like Nurcholish Madjid, Azyumardi Azra, and Abdurrahman Wahid, who "combine an intimate familiarity with the Islamic tradition with an equally solid knowledge of recent achievements of the Western academe in the human sciences" (ibid., 90).

Like Kersten, I see these new Muslim intellectuals as cosmopolitan from the perspectives of "attitude or disposition" and "practice or competence" (Vertovec and Cohen 2002, 7). Characterized by cultural hybridity (Tomlinson 1999), these intellectuals have not only "a willingness to engage with the Other" but also the skill to "make one's way into other cultures [and to] maneuver . . . more or less expertly with a particular system of meaning and meaningful forms" (Hannerz 1990, 239). In short, cosmopolitanism must "include a stance towards diversity itself, toward the coexistence of cultures in the individual experience" (ibid., 239).

In the Malay Archipelago, a region with hundreds of coexisting cultures, such a stance toward diversity would seemingly be taken for granted. Indonesia's national motto, "Bhinneka Tunggal Ika" (literally "different but still one"), celebrates unity in diversity. But in the realm of religion, the word *pluralism* is problematic, as for conservative Muslims the implication that all religions are equally valid violates the belief that Islam is the one true religion and should thus rule supreme (Burhani 2013, 111). If historian David Hollinger (2002, 231) is right that cosmopolitanism is marked by the will to engage human diversity, and the expectation that individuals will be simultaneously affiliated with a number of groups while at the same time encouraging "the voluntary formation of new communities of wider scope," then many of the Muslim journalists at the news organizations represented in this book have been quietly and consistently practicing cosmopolitanism all along.

Muslim scholars have argued that there is significant justification for press freedom in Islam, contending that the principles of commanding good and forbidding evil, sincere advice, consultation, independent reasoning, and the right to criticize government leaders are each premised on the recognition of freedom of expression that is basic to the sharia, or divine law of Islam (Kamali 2002, 26). Although journalists interviewed in Indonesia and

Malaysia frequently referred to passages from the Qur'an in talking about their day-to-day work, their knowledge of Islam is not the focus of this book nor is the accuracy of their interpretation. Rather, its concern is with how Muslim journalists anchor the meaning of their work in a context of Islam and what that means for the kind of journalism they practice.

POLITICAL VALUES, JOURNALISTS' VALUES

As emeritus professor of Islamic studies Seyyed Hossein Nasr (2002, 3) writes, the "heart of Islam," as expressed in the *shahada*, is oneness (called *tawhid*). *Tawhid* is "beyond all duality and relationality" and "the axis around which all that is Islamic revolves." In Islam the oneness of God means that the community's political well-being is not a "distraction" from religion but the "stuff of religion itself" (Armstrong 2002, xi). The fundamental goals of Islam—a just society in which all members are treated with respect—are part of a totality, a path that encompasses all aspects of life.

In Western democracies, journalism is generally understood to be a secular occupation. In the United States, popular understanding of the role of the press is rooted in the ideas of the Enlightenment and the doctrine of natural rights (Levy 1985). American journalists' understanding of press freedom grew out of this Enlightenment model, in which the press is seen as a defender of the people against the arbitrary power of the state (Bailyn 1967). In Islamic political thought, by contrast, both legal and moral values are determined by divine revelation. Afghan Islamic scholar Mohammad Hashim Kamali (1998) explains that unlike modern constitutional law, the sharia is inspired by the unity of God and man. "Islamic law does not proceed from a position of conflict between the respective rights or interests of the individual and state.... [T]hus the duality of interest which is often envisaged in modern constitutions does not present the same picture as in the Islamic theory of government" (ibid., 18). Because of this, many occupations that would be considered in the West to be in the social or political sphere are understood in Islamic societies to have a religious component, even if at an unconscious level.

Most of the scholarly research on journalism and Islam focuses either on media in the Arab world or journalism in the Middle East, with particular attention to *Al Jazeera* (Amin 2002; Pintak and Ginges 2008; Seib 2008). For example, in 2002, media scholar Hussein Amin (2002, 127) painted a grim picture of the state of Arab journalism, arguing that "the political culture of the Arab world determines the success or failure" of its media. Marked by censorship and domination by one political party, the entire region has suffered from a lack of press freedom and media independence. Concluding that at the end of the millennium, Arab journalists "continue[d] to be victims of harassment and political pressures, including dismissal, censorship, restraints on travel, physical assault, threats, arrest, detention, torture, abduction, passport withdrawals, and exile," Amin (ibid., 127) argued that government penetration in all sectors of society hindered the development of a free press. Noting that national media policies in the Arab world "reinforce cultural and national traditions and values," Amin (ibid., 129) pointed to a general sensitivity toward criticism enshrined in many penal codes that expressly prohibits criticism of the state, political officials, the military, or religious leaders. Touching lightly on the political culture of Islam, Amin (ibid., 129) added that "most Arab journalists defend Islamic societies, traditions and values in general" and that "freedom of expression does not include offensive or negative statements about Islam or religious beliefs."

This geographical bias with regard to journalism is related to the equally biased focus on Islamic practices in the Arab world, as if Islam and the culture of Arabs were one and the same. Writing a few years later, media scholar Lawrence Pintak and psychologist Jeremy Ginges (2008, 193) found in a cross-border survey of 601 Arab journalists that a majority "see their mission as that of driving political and social reform in the Middle East and North Africa." Yet, significantly, Pintak also noted differences in the ways that journalists in these countries view their profession and that these differences "can be explained by an array of political, social and economic factors within the regions studied, such as the form of government and level of political stability, the presence or absence of conflict, and the state of the economy" (Pintak 2013, 498). Political scientist Philip Howard (2011, 33) has likewise noted in his study of the role of the internet in transitions to democracies in Muslim countries that "technology diffusion has become, *in combination with other factors* both a necessary and sufficient cause of democratic transition or entrenchment" (emphasis added).

By focusing on the Arab experience and Arab media, most existing research on journalism and Islam ignores media in Southeast Asia. Not only is this bias misleading, it also overlooks the 13 percent of the world's Muslims that live in Malaysia and Indonesia—the latter of which is the world's most populous Muslim-majority country. There are exceptions to this geographical bias, and some of the most recent and significant work in the area of journalism and Islam in Indonesia has been that of coauthors Lawrence Pintak and Budi Setiyono (2011), who, with a team of Indonesian researchers, surveyed hundreds of Indonesian journalists with regard to their views on identity, religion, and journalistic values.

Despite the comprehensiveness of Pintak and Setiyono's survey, the weaknesses of survey research are well known. Although the journalists' responses to the survey questions were consistent with my findings, their answers necessarily lack context and nuance. Although my pool of informants is much smaller, I have their trust—as well as nearly twenty years of detailed interview transcripts, many of which are listed in this book's bibliography. Even though I began to focus on journalism and Islam only five or six years ago, it has been present in my research since 1999. In fact, the first inkling I got of the relationship between the two occurred when I was just beginning my study of *Tempo* magazine. Ulil Abshar-Abdalla—at that time a young scholar and today one of Indonesia's leading theorists of "liberal Islam"—suggested that *Tempo*'s most important contribution may have been the role it played in publicizing what would later become known as the "renewal in Islamic thinking."

In their book *Challenging Authoritarianism in Southeast Asia*, editors Ariel Heryanto and Sumit K. Mandal (2003, 11) noted that when in 1997 they first conceptualized a comparative study of Indonesia and Malaysia, "it was not easy to advance a rationale" for the project. Within just one year, as Indonesia's President Soeharto was forced to step down and the call for *reformasi* spread across the Straits to Malaysia, this reluctance to examine the two countries in a comparative context would seem odd.

Indonesia and Malaysia have a great deal in common, including language, religion, and culture, and are often described as two peoples who are "*serumpun*" (sharing the same roots). In addition to shared ethnocultural identities, there has, in the post-Soekarno/Confrontation era, been a sense of "blood brotherhood" and a willingness for active engagement between Jakarta and Kuala Lumpur so that " '*pisang jangan berbuah dua kali*' (never again should there be confrontation between these two peoples of the same stock)" (Liow 2003, 350). Yet these surface similarities mask profound differences, in many cases dating back to colonial-era rule. These differing histories and political cultures of Indonesia and Malaysia also influence the ways that journalists think about their work. Such factors as the legacy of colonial rule, the development of the early nationalist press, the politicization of religion, the locus of religious authority, and the role of the state affect the ways that journalism is practiced and understood.

Most scholarly work on journalism in Indonesia and Malaysia has focused either on individual publications (Steele 2005; Tarrant 2008), the overall press system (Hill 1994; Romano 2003), or the transition to democracy (Hill and Sen 2011; Williams and Rich 2000). Although there is a growing literature on Islam and democracy in Indonesia (Tomsa 2010; Hefner 2000), there has been little study of ordinary day-to-day journalism as it is understood and practiced by Muslim professionals in these countries.

METHOD

Since sociologist Herbert Gans (1979) undertook his study of CBS, NBC, and *Newsweek* magazines and wrote about how American journalists "decide what's news," there has been little replication of his work overseas. Gans used a combination of quantitative and qualitative methods to examine how the nation and society are depicted in American journalism. Beyond this, he determined the "enduring values" that suffuse news reports. In the case of the United States, these values include ethnocentrism, altruistic democracy, responsible capitalism, and individualism (ibid., 42). Although the work of Gans is now nearly forty years old, his approach is still the gold standard of newsroom ethnography. His combination of observation, interviews, and close textual analysis enabled him to write with confidence of the enduring values of American journalism.

I take the same approach to understanding the enduring values that underlie journalism in Southeast Asia. My research is primarily ethnographic and historical, drawing upon twenty years of research and teaching in Indonesia and Malaysia.[1] It uses interviews and participant observation at five publications, each representing a different relationship between journalism and Islam. In Jakarta most of my time has been spent at the newsweekly *Tempo*, where, since 1999, I have regularly observed and attended Wednesday editorial meetings. Beginning with a sabbatical in 2012–13, I have also spent considerable time at *Republika*, a newspaper founded to serve the Muslim community. Although the Islamist magazine *Sabili* was in decline when I began this research, I have known Herry Nurdi, its most famous editor, since 2004. Herry has been generous not only with his time but also with his goodwill, inviting me to teach workshops and introducing me to his colleagues, thus opening the door to further meetings and interviews. In Malaysia, *Malaysiakini*'s chief editor Steven Gan has allowed me the use of a desk at the online news portal since 2008 and included me in many meetings and retreats. More recently, the editors of *Harakah* and *HarakahDaily .net*, the publications of Malaysia's Islamic party, have given me access to their newsrooms and allowed me to teach courses there.

The advantages of ethnography are well known: careful observation of communities from the inside can lead to nuanced interpretations and multidimensional analyses of practices and belief systems that would otherwise be unavailable. The pitfalls are equally obvious: not only can access be a problem but the interpreter also risks influencing the communities that he or she is studying. I am lucky in that I have had extraordinary access to the news organizations under consideration. To me, fieldwork is a series of reciprocal relationships; I am always willing to teach writing workshops, consult about study abroad, and write letters of recommendation for fellowships. Whenever possible, I also bring cookies. Careful nurturing of these relationships has allowed me to build the trust required to observe and inquire about practices and beliefs that would not be obvious from either surveys or brief interviews. Finally, what I have learned about journalism and Islam during my fieldwork has been supported by what I've observed in journalism courses offered by Islamic universities and institutes in both Indonesia and Malaysia, some of which I discuss in the book's conclusion. For students and members of the faculties of these institutions, the connections between the principles of journalism and the teachings of Islam are obvious (Steele 2012).

THE PRINCIPLES OF JOURNALISM, THE TEACHINGS OF ISLAM

There are recurring patterns in what Muslim journalists in Indonesia and Malaysia say about the meaning of their work, even at publications that do not claim to be "Islamic." Although when I began my research many of my sources assumed that I was studying threats to freedom of expression from religious conservatives, once I explained that my real interest was in the relationship between the values of journalism and the teachings of Islam, they generally responded in the language of religion. For example, as former *Indonesia Raya* managing editor Atmakusumah Astraatmadja said, the goal of journalism "is to reach for goodness": "In our book, *Mochtar Lubis,*

Wartawan Jihad [Mochtar Lubis, jihad journalist] we called *Indonesia Raya* a jihad newspaper. To reach for justice, for goodness, for progress, that's what journalism is. Yes, unconsciously, since we were little, we learned this [vocabulary of Islam] in school. We studied Islam. And I don't see a difference between our religion and journalism. It's exactly parallel. *Jihad* can be a war, but it can also be a struggle for self-defense, for justice, for truth. It's the same. There is no difference with Islam." *Malaysiakini*'s Fathi Aris Omar similarly said: "In terms of ethics, journalism is almost 100 percent the same as the goals of religion: to seek justice, to help the poor, to promote equal distribution of wealth, and to fight against corruption."

Journalists in Indonesia and Malaysia are well versed in Western notions of the principles of journalism as well as in what makes journalism "good." In Indonesia the Dr. Soetomo Press Institute has been conducting trainings in the basics of journalism since its establishment in 1988. Goenawan Mohamad's Institute for the Study of the Free-Flow of Information (Institut Studi Arus Informasi, ISAI) has received USAID funding to assist in the development of press freedom (Steele 2005). ISAI and the Pantau Institute in Jakarta translated American press critics Bill Kovach and Tom Rosenstiel's *Elements of Journalism* (2001) with a grant from the US Department of State, and have conducted trainings throughout the Indonesian archipelago. In Malaysia the government-supported Malaysian Press Institute offers basic and advanced training for journalists, and the politically independent news organization *Malaysiakini* has received multiple grants from the US Department of State to conduct trainings for citizen journalists. But when journalists in Indonesia and Malaysia speak about such basic elements of journalism as truth, balance, verification, and independence from power, what exactly do they mean?

Muslim journalists in Indonesia and Malaysia often illustrate the fundamental principles of journalism with verses from the Qur'an, or examples from the Hadith. For example, when asked about the relationship between his faith and his work, former *Jawa Pos* editor Dhimam Abror began with the Qur'anic obligation to tell others the truth: "We believe that the Prophet Muhammad says if you get from me only one verse from the Qur'an, you have an obligation to tell that verse to other people. I think that yes, *dakwah* [propagation] in the biggest understanding is *dakwah* in front of many people, but *dakwah* in the smallest understanding is that if you only know one verse from the Qur'an, you have an obligation to tell it to other people."

When asked if there was a connection between his work and his faith as a Muslim, former *Tempo* journalist Yusi Avianto Pareanom likewise focused on the importance of truth, which the American Committee of Concerned Journalists referred to as a journalist's "first obligation":

> I am seldom asked why I became a journalist. At a time when I was much younger, it is one of our duties, *tabligh*, to spread words, or to share. The Prophet was given revelation. But he didn't just get God's word, he also delivered the message. Now, spreading the word, I don't think that we are like the Prophet, but I'm a part of that kind of process and that makes me happy, you know? And according to me, that's interesting. Because you cannot achieve the highest status of the Prophet, but at least you can work in the same area. [Laughs].

The notion of balance can likewise be seen as Islamic. As in English, a synonym for balance in news is "fair," which both Indonesians and Malaysians translate as *adil* (just). Not only is justice (*keadilan*) a principle theme of the Qur'an, it is also a fundamental concept in journalism. Sociologist Gaye Tuchman (1972, 665) has shown that the presentation of conflicting possibilities is one element of the "strategic ritual of objectivity" and this news norm is widely recognized in both Indonesia and Malaysia, where it is generally referred to (in English) as "covering both sides." Like balance, verification is often described by journalists in Islamic terms. During five years spent studying the relationship between Islam and journalism, the Qur'anic verse that I have heard cited most frequently is this one: "O believers, if an evildoer comes to you with some news, verify it (investigate to ascertain the truth), lest you should harm others unwittingly and then regret what you have done" (Qur'an, "Al-Hujuraat" 49:6 [Malik translation]).

Journalists often describe the process of *isnad*, or verifying "the chain of transmission" of the words and deeds of the Prophet Muhammad as being similar to the journalistic principle of verification. Indonesian Islamic university lecturer Faris Khairul Anam (2009, 57) explicitly connects *isnad* with the process of journalistic verification in *Fikih Jurnalistik* (Journalistic jurisprudence), noting that when a journalist hears a story, he or she must ask, "Who said that? From where did you hear about this?" Mohammad Hashim Kamali (2002, 23), of the International Institute of Advanced Islamic Studies (IAIS) in Malaysia, provides numerous examples from the Qur'an and the Hadith of the importance of speaking truth to power, including the Prophet's statement that "the best form of jihad is to tell a word of truth to an oppressive ruler." Indonesian journalists frequently mention this passage—as well as the sayings of the first two caliphs that the people should correct them if they deviate from the truth—to support their conviction that it is wrong to support a despot, even if that despot is nominally Muslim. The view that one is obligated to challenge an oppressive ruler is one that is, perhaps not surprisingly, also heard from Muslim journalists who work at Malaysia's alternative media, including *Harakah* and *Malaysiakini*.

Although scholars have long debated whether there is a uniquely "Islamic" form of communication, for journalism faculty at Indonesia's state Islamic universities and institutes, as well as for their counterparts at the International Islamic University of Malaysia, there is no question that for Muslims, Islamic journalism has to be different from—and better than—ordinary journalism. Discussions with faculty at these universities and institutes suggest that for Muslim journalists, journalism should be inspirational and "prophetic." Lecturers at each of the Indonesian universities and institutes I visited have written short books for use in class, and many of these works make explicit the connection between journalism and Islam. One such book, used at UIN Sunan Kalijaga in Yogyakarta and simply titled *Jurnalistik*, defines the mission of Islamic journalism as news "with an important meaning" (Daulay, Rifa'I, Akhmad, and Musthofa 2006, 64). According to the authors, Islamic journalism has to be interesting, honest, and true. The facts must be credible and consistent with the mission of *amar ma'ruf nahi munkar*, or inviting good and forbidding evil. For the authors the mission could not be more clear: Islamic journalism should have the characteristics of Islamic teachings.

At the Indonesian newspaper *Republika*, which was established in 1993 to serve the Muslim community (Utomo 2010), the connections between the values of good journalism and the teachings of Islam are made explicit. When Syahruddin El Fikri, one of the newspaper's assistant managing editors, teaches new recruits the meaning of "Islamic journalism," he gives them a handout on journalistic ethics and feature writing that includes a list of verses from the Qur'an that are relevant to the work of journalists. The handout concludes that journalism is a "noble" profession and something that is "very much in keeping with Islamic values":

There are many other verses of both the Qur'an and the Hadith of the
Prophet that order the Islamic community to behave honestly, not to lie, to
help those who are weak, not to take what doesn't belong to them, and other
things like that.

Because of this, I believe that truly all writing that's done by journalists
is work that is very Islamic. Whatever the media is—just as long as the
writing doesn't spread lies, slander, sex, etc. (El Fikri 2010, 10)

Like many of his colleagues at *Republika*, Syahruddin emphasizes that the teachings of Islam require that Muslim journalists adhere to higher standards than those of their non-Muslim counterparts. For example, while all journalists are trained to avoid libel (*fitnah*), Muslim journalists have an additional obligation to steer clear of gossip and backbiting (*ghibah*), which in the Qur'an is likened to eating the flesh of one's dead brother.[2]

Even Muslim journalists in Indonesia and Malaysia who work for media that are generally not considered to be "Islamic" talk about the *meaning* of journalism in terms that reflect religious values. *Tempo*'s current chief editor Arif Zulkifli, who was involved in the student missionary or *dakwah* movement in the 1980s, says that he does not see his current work as a journalist as a kind of *dakwah*. Yet despite his insistence that Islamic values have nothing to do with journalism, Arif Zulkifli's (2009) explanation of the significance of his work suggests otherwise: "I believe that I'm in this world to gather goodness. I have to do lots of good things, or 'invite good and forbid evil' so that later, when I die, it won't all have been for nothing. I believe in life after death. I believe that each person will be held accountable. I am perhaps not a good Muslim in terms of having a ritual; I am not perfect in that regard. But I believe that what I write, what I report, what I have done for *Tempo* are good things that I can be proud of after I die."

JOURNALISM, POLITICS, AND DEMOCRACY

While most non-Muslims are aware of the Shia-Sunni fault line that divides the Muslim world, there are others too—including the one dividing the democracies from the authoritarian regimes. This fault line also divides Indonesia and Malaysia, the latter of which is in many ways more typical of the Islamic world in that power and the state are fused with religious authority. Although there are cultural similarities between Malaysia and Indonesia, there are key differences in political structures. In Malaysia, aside from its semiauthoritarian democracy (Crouch 1996), the state is involved in religious affairs to an extent that is unimaginable in Indonesia. Although the rights of different categories of citizens are enshrined in Article 3 of the Constitution, the official religion of Malaysia is Islam, and the state has the last word on matters of religion. Because Malays are Muslim by definition and thus required to adhere to sharia, in practice freedom of religion for Malays is limited to choices within Islam. This level of state involvement, in addition to the more recent politicization of Islam, has had profound implications for the ways that Muslims and non-Muslims interact even in otherwise pluralist spaces.

The colonial and postcolonial histories of Indonesia and Malaysia—as with much of the Muslim world—have made Indonesians and Malaysians profoundly skeptical of "liberalism," which is associated with capitalism, exploitation, and uneven economic development that benefits the first world at the expense of the third. These concerns echo those of the Islamic reform movement associated with Al-Azhar Sheik Muhammad 'Abduh over one hundred years ago, when students from Malaya and the Indies likewise struggled with injustice and the question of why the Muslim world was bound by the shackles of colonialism.

The struggle for economic justice and protection of the weak are not only fundamental to Islam (Azlan 2005), they are also "enduring values" in the practice of journalism in Indonesia and Malaysia (Steele 2005; Steele 2011). As *Tempo* magazine's founding editor Goenawan Mohamad once said, "It is very difficult in Indonesia if you don't speak about justice. Indonesian history is the history of searching for justice, more than searching for freedom" (quoted in Steele 2005, 23). Toriq Hadad, a former chief editor of *Tempo*, likewise noted that "the mission of *Tempo* is justice" (ibid., 23).

Muslims are far more motivated by the goal of justice than they are by freedom. In Islam, rulers and subjects alike are bound by certain obligations toward one another. In the case of the ruled, these obligations include obedience to those in authority. Yet the authority of rulers is not unlimited. If those in authority violate the law, or if their rule is "illegitimate or unjust," they may forfeit their claim to obedience (Lewis 1988, 91–92). Scholars have argued that in Islam, "forbidding wrong" is paramount and that Muslims have an obligation to stop evil when they see it (Cook 2003). In the Hadith (secondary report of the Prophet Muhammad's actions, words, and even silence that is also believed to be inspired by God) the Prophet is quoted as saying: "Whoever sees a wrong, and is able to put it right . . . with his hand, let him do so; if he can't, then with his tongue; if he can't, then in his heart, and that is the bare minimum of faith" (quoted in ibid. 2003, 4).

In Indonesia and Malaysia the watchdog role of the press is grounded not in liberalism but rather the obligation of Muslims to stop evil when they see it. In Malaysia we see this in *Harakah*'s scathing critiques of the greed and corruption of the ruling Barisan Nasional (National Front) coalition. For much of Indonesian press history, "evil" was likewise related to the political context of Soeharto's New Order, an unjust political system in which there were virtually no limits to the government's authority. This lack of justice led *Tempo* magazine writers to lend subtle support to ordinary people in their struggle against the overwhelming power of the state (Steele 2005). The goal of Muslim journalists to expose corruption among political elites is thus the same as that of Western watchdog journalism—but the means of getting there is different. They have internalized the teaching of commanding right and forbidding wrong in such a way that it unconsciously governs how they view their obligations as journalists, just as their American counterparts have internalized a different understanding of the rights of journalists as guardians of the liberties of the people.

In the late 1970s, Herbert Gans wrote that the "paraideology" of Western journalism was reform, a liberal set of values that grew out of the Progressive Era. Because of the demonization of liberalism, we will not find these same justifications in Islamic journalism, yet the paraideology of justice reinforces a set of values that are essentially liberal—although they are not ordinarily seen as such. Thus the story of the modern journalisms of Islam is that which is familiar and liberal set off against that which is deeply Islamic.

Many years ago, I gave a series of talks on doing good journalism at the Malaysian National News Agency, Bernama. After the formal lecture, a group of young journalists asked how they could practice good journalism in a society in which there was so much government control. I told them what the Indonesian journalist and intellectual Arief Budiman had said years ago when I was working on my *Tempo* book. "In Islam," he said, "we have this kind of saying. If you see something bad happening, you have to stop it with your hands. If you cannot stop it with your hands, stop it with your mouth. If you cannot stop it with your mouth, stop it with your heart."Arief went on to conclude that "different people have different capacities," and "we don't want always to ask people to do something with their hands. . . . But at least we want people to stop with their heart. That means they are not betraying their consciences." I was astonished at how much Arief's comments resonated, especially given that these young Bernama journalists were employed by the Malaysian government news agency. Of course, as I later learned, this was not just "a saying" but rather a teaching that is essential to Islam. Related to the commandment to enjoin good and forbid evil, it is the cardinal principle by which citizens are entitled to "forbid, whether in words, acts, or silent denunciation, any evil which they see being committed" (Kamali 2002, 28). For journalists, who live by the word, the applications are obvious.

The notion of press freedom does not resonate in the majority-Muslim societies of Indonesia and Malaysia in the same way that it does in the West. As *Tempo*'s Toriq Hadad said, "Press freedom, this is a Western definition." Referring to a newspaper that was affiliated with then-president Susilo Bambang Yudhoyono's [SBY's] Democratic party, he added: "*Jurnal Nasional* is very free, they can write about anything! But if they want to write about SBY, what is possible?" Pointing to the difference between media that are "free" and media that are "independent," Toriq noted that although journalists who work for the *Jurnal Nasional* may be free to write whatever they want about the president, "they are only going to write what is good. So they are not independent in the matter of SBY." Although Muslim journalists in Indonesia and Malaysia may not be moved by the goal of freedom, they understand the importance of speaking truth to power and of stopping what is wrong with their words. The modern history of both Indonesia and Malaysia suggests that without independent media, justice is no more possible than either freedom or democracy.

THE FIVE PUBLICATIONS

For scholars of religion, the fact that there have been and continue to be endless debates about what Islam is and how it should be practiced is not surprising. Scholars of communication, however, might be surprised to learn how many of these debates have found their way into journalism. The five publications—three from Indonesia, two from Malaysia—each represent different aspects of Islam and hence different aspects of journalism. Although one is owned by a political party, it is a party of the opposition; thus each of the five publications is independent from the state.[3] Editors of the five publications are aware of one another, and their histories intersect in interesting ways.

For *Sabili* magazine, influenced by the *tarbiyah* or education movement, authentic Islam is drawn from the Qur'an and the Hadith as well as from the example of the *salaf as-saaleh* (pious predecessors) who were the first Muslims (Rijal 2005, 437). Any practice that departed from these basic texts—particularly local Indonesian traditions and the views of "liberal" Muslims—was considered deviant and thus unacceptable to the editors and writers of *Sabili*, which went out of business in April 2013. For *Republika* newspaper, established by the Indonesian Muslim Intellectuals' Association (ICMI) with the blessing of then-President Soeharto and now owned by a large corporation with many business interests, the Muslim community is a market, and Islam is a market niche. Since its sale to Mahaka Media in 2000, *Republika* has tried not to offend its large and mostly middle-class readership, and the articles it presents on Islam tend to appeal to the Muslim mainstream.

For *Tempo* magazine and newspaper, it is pluralism that is important, not Islam. Despite the fact that the vast majority of *Tempo* journalists are Muslim, the conviction that *Tempo* has nothing to do with Islam was repeated by every editor or reporter I interviewed. Despite this certainty, *Tempo* has, since its founding in 1971, given space to progressive Muslim intellectuals who have called for a renewal in Islamic thinking—including most recently Jaringan Islam Liberal (JIL, the Liberal Islamic Network). As a nondenominational news organization, *Tempo* thus gives voice to an approach to Islam that can best be described as cosmopolitan.

In Malaysia, *Harakah* is the paper of the Islamist party PAS (Parti Islam Se-Malaysia, the Pan-Malaysian Islamic party). Journalists at the newspaper and the online edition of the paper have worked hard to reconcile the principles of journalism with the teachings of Islam and the needs of their political party. Despite the many possible pitfalls, the paper has for many years been led by journalists of striking ability—and by what at first blush appears to be a surprising commitment to press freedom.[4] One of the key questions that comes up with any study of Islamist political movements is how compatible is the goal of the Islamic state with democratic institutions? Is it possible to imagine an Islamic state that claims, with the Muslim Brotherhood, that "Islam is the solution" while at the same time promoting participatory rights for non-Muslims as well as basic freedom of expression and of the press? The experiences of *Harakah* and *HarakahDaily.net* offer some insights.

Malaysiakini, the online news portal, is not Islamic at all. Editor Steven Gan keeps discussions of religion out of the newsroom and opposes even the use of the word *secular* to describe *Malaysiakini*, as it implies a focus on religion with which he is not comfortable. Yet despite *Malaysiakini*'s nonconfessional stance, approximately one-third of its journalists are Malay and Muslim. How they negotiate this identity—mandated by Malaysian law—while nevertheless maintaining their commitment to pursuing the truth is one of the more interesting stories of alternative media in Malaysia.

Despite their major differences, these five news organizations share a common history; in some ways they are also *serumpun*, in a sense of having shared roots. *Tempo, Sabili,* and *Republika* were each founded during Soeharto's New Order (1966–98) and had to develop strategies for survival under an authoritarian regime known for its tightly controlled press. The regime justified these repressive regulations by pointing to the necessity of restoring order and maintaining stability. One aspect of this stability was managing a multicultural society and controlling those who argued in favor of an Islamic state. Two of the publications I examine, *Tempo* and *Sabili,* were ultimately shut down by the regime, albeit for very different reasons. *Republika* survived, but only because it had the protection of B. J. Habibie, minister of research and technology, who was both the founder of ICMI and a close associate of President Soeharto.

With the fall of Soeharto in 1998 and the rise of *reformasi*, both *Tempo* and *Sabili* came back to print and *Republika* lost its patron. The push for democratic reform echoed across the Straits of Malacca and inspired many in Malaysia as well. Young Malay Muslim editors at *Harakah*, the paper of the Islamic party PAS, were especially taken with the possibilities proclaimed by Indonesian Muslim intellectuals such as Amien Rais, who was a member of the editorial board and a regular columnist at *Republika*. The sacking of Anwar Ibrahim, Malaysian deputy prime minister, in 1998 led to the Malaysian political movement that was also called *reformasi*, and inspired a number of new websites and blogs, one of which was *Malaysiakini*. Although *Malaysiakini* was steadfastly independent of *reformasi*, it was nevertheless a child of it, sharing the movement's commitment to human rights and democratic reform.

Meanwhile, an end to the restrictive regulations on establishing a print publication in Indonesia brought both *Tempo* and *Sabili* back to print. If under Soeharto the owners of print publications had functioned as a sort of cartel, the new market forces unleashed in the reform era meant that *Republika* could no longer rely on ICMI for patronage and had to search for a new owner. The resulting shake-up led not only to new ownership but also to an exodus of journalists, many of whom ended up at *Tempo* newspaper, to which they brought an understanding of "*Islam kosmopolitan.*" This more progressive orientation raised the ire of literalist Muslims at *Sabili*, who made it their enemy.

"ISLAM IS A WAY OF LIFE"

This book is about journalism, but it is also about Islam. It is not about the theology of Islam, but rather about a set of practices. It is not about what Islam is, but rather about what Muslims do. Whereas *Sabili* called itself "Islamic" and *Harakah* is the voice of an Islamic party, there are also journalists at *Tempo* and *Malaysiakini* who are strict in their practice of Islamic teachings and view their work as journalists within an Islamic context. So who should define which media and approaches to journalism are "Islamic"? Although there is no agreement on the relationship between journalism and Islam, all Muslim journalists see themselves as pursuing the truth.

Sabili is the most politically conservative of the publications and represents a perspective that was hobbled by the Soeharto regime but roared back to power with the rise of *reformasi* and an open media system.[5] *Republika* newspaper has focused on Islam as a market niche and reflects a popular piety that attracts both advertisers and Indonesia's growing middle class. *Harakah*, the newspaper of the Malaysian political party PAS, has struggled to balance the principles of journalism, the teachings of Islam, and the often competing interests of party elites. Malaysia's online news portal *Malaysiakini* strives to negotiate the course of race and religion while at the same time providing critical coverage of the government. Finally, *Tempo* is known for its cosmopolitanism, reflected in its focus on the liberal/progressive ideas that were centered first in the Islamic "renewal" movement of Islamic scholar Nurcholish Madjid and more recently in its championing of the Liberal Islamic Network.

These five examples suggest that our definition of Islamic journalism has been too narrow. Despite the popular misconceptions about journalism and Islam—even within Indonesia and Malaysia—Muslim journalists take a variety of approaches to their work. A focus on how Muslim journalists from five very different publications in Indonesia and Malaysia understand the meaning of their work thus suggests not only contending views of the relationship between journalism and Islam but also a richness of experience that has been overlooked by scholars of journalism. In a world in which Islam is often seen as antithetical to democracy, it is important to understand that publications that defend pluralism while fighting for justice and defending the rights of the weak can be run by journalists who are neither liberal nor "secular." This different approach should not be seen as a sort of halfway point to the "real" way of doing journalism; it is rather how many Muslim professionals understand and explain their work.

ONE

SABILI

Scripturalist Islam

"ARE YOU going to write a book about me?" Eman Mulyatman is a slight man with a prayer bump on his forehead. He was the last editor of *Sabili* magazine, which folded in April 2013, and we are in the Food Hall café in the basement of the Puri Casablanca apartments in Kuningan, Jakarta. It is Ramadan, and we are waiting to break the fast. Eman is wearing the purple batik shirt he had worn to Friday prayers, and he keeps looking over his shoulder to see if any of the other customers are listening.

"No," I say. "I'm a scholar, and I'm writing about the principles of journalism and the teachings of Islam." We are both thinking of Sadanand Dhume's 2009 *My Friend the Fanatic*, a book about Herry Nurdi, another former editor of *Sabili*, who is a mutual friend. Dhume hired Herry as his fixer, then wrote a book in which Herry became the main character. Although the book added to Herry's already considerable fame, it also brought him notoriety and accusations that he was "Intel" or perhaps even working for the CIA. Although Eman's paranoia seems excessive, it is typical of *Sabili*, a magazine with a history rife with intrigue and rumors of infiltration at the highest level. As an Islamist publication that openly called for the implementation of sharia and defended the interests of Muslims from the Moluccas to the Palestinian Territories, it is not surprising that *Sabili* attracted the attention of Indonesian government authorities.

Sabili is a difficult publication about which to write. The kind of Islam it represents has been called scripturalist, literalist, and even fundamentalist (Liddle 1996b, 271).[1] There are at least three different aspects of the Islamist magazine that make for intersecting storylines: journalism, politics, and intrigue. Although the magazine's politics—variously described as "sensational," "provocative," and prone to offering "Zionist-crusader conspiracy theor[ies]" (Lim 2005, 23)—have garnered considerable attention, the publication has not been examined in terms of how its editors and reporters viewed the practice of journalism. Despite its provocative nature—which included naming Abu Bakar Ba'asyir, the man widely believed to be the spiritual inspiration for the Bali bombers, its 2002 "man of the year"—at least some of the magazine's editors thought seriously about journalism.[2] It could be argued, in fact, that *Sabili* actually had the most fully developed theory of journalism and Islam of any of the publications under consideration, although it did not always live up to its own principles.

ISLAM IN INDONESIA

In Indonesia the role of the state in matters of religion is significantly different from that of Malaysia. As Islamic law expert M. B. Hooker (2003, 12) has asserted, the Dutch "thoroughly misunderstood Islam," seeing it as a tightly organized hierarchical religion similar to Roman Catholicism. Historian Harry J. Benda (1958, 19) has argued that in Indonesia, the Dutch were more concerned with rebellion than they were with regulating Islam: "These fears had helped to shape a policy of alliance with those elements in Indonesian society—particular the princes and *priyayi* on Java, and sultans, rajahs, and *adat*-chiefs on the other islands—who for political reasons of their own were known to be either lukewarm Muslims or outright enemies of Islamic 'fanaticism.'" It wasn't until 1889, when Christiaan Snouck Hurgronje was appointed adviser on Arabian and Native Affairs that the Dutch began to reassess their policies.

Snouck worked to assuage Dutch fears by distinguishing between Islam as a religion and as a political force. Arguing that the Dutch had nothing to fear from Islam as a religion, Snouck counseled in favor of toleration for Muslim religious life. Yet at the same time, he called for a policy of vigilance against "all those trends that bear, or tend to bear, a political character" (Benda 1958, 24). In Snouck's view, modernization was the key to managing Islam in Indonesia. This would be attained primarily through education and by making the *priyayi* elites active participants in Dutch culture and social life. The policy enjoyed limited success. In the Dutch East Indies, both sharia judges and the rural ulama were isolated from elite centers of power—a situation that would have profound implications for the role of

Islam in postcolonial Indonesia. Whereas in British Malaya state religious authorities were given power to punish "Muhammadan offenses" such as public fast-breaking during Ramadan, gambling, and failure to attend Friday prayers, in the Indies "Islamic leadership wanted to divorce all spheres of Islamic life from Dutch control" (Yeger 1979, 264). Far from being co-opted, in the Indies the ulama were a counterweight to state power and control.

As Hooker (2003, 14) has noted, Indonesian nationalists had little sympathy for the Muslim cause, seeing it as a threat to future independence. In their view the Muslim position was "peasant-based and out of sympathy with socialist and liberal ideologies." Although in the closing days of the Japanese occupation a coalition of Muslim organizations advocated that the constitution would contain words stipulating that "enacting the Sharia was incumbent on all Muslim citizens," Soekarno's more pluralist view prevailed (Laffan 2003, 407). These words, which became known as the Jakarta Charter, continue to this day to resonate in Indonesian Islamist political ideology.

Although a full discussion of the Islamic state debate is outside the parameters of this book, it is important to note that the debate itself dates back to the 1930s and 1940s, with secular nationalists such as Soekarno supporting the separation between religion and state, and modernist Muslims such as Mohammad Natsir opposing it (Hooker 2003, 30). In 1945 the ideology of Pancasila was accepted as a necessary compromise between the Muslim parties' desire for an Islamic state and secular-nationalist concerns that non-Muslims from the "outer islands" would leave the young republic. The compromise was neither Islamic nor fully secular. As theologian Karel Steenbrink (1999, 281) has argued, the first of the five principles, belief in "Ketuhanan yang Maha Esa," should be translated as "One Superior Deity" rather than as the more personal concept of God. Although Pancasila became a means of keeping together the unlikely Nasakom coalition of the Nationalist, Muslim, and Communist parties during the years of Soekarno's "Guided Democracy," many Muslims felt that their opponents used the ideology as a weapon to weaken Islam.

Under Soeharto's New Order, Pancasila became an "official, civil religion" (ibid., 281). In 1984, the year that *Sabili* was founded, five government-sponsored laws required Pancasila to be the sole basis for all social and political organizations, including religious ones (Hefner 2000). Thus, as Southeast Asia specialist Lili Yulyadi Arnakim (2011) has argued, the debate over the Islamic state/nationalist state had come full circle. "Suharto's containment policy to control political Islam was in effect identical to what was advocated by Snouck Hurgronje: to separate Islam from politics. If Hurgronje tried to preempt the creation of an Islamic political leadership, the Suharto government was to destroy the leadership and, secondly, to turn Muslims away from Islamist politics and ideology" (ibid., 51).

Indonesia is home to several important Muslim organizations, including the world's largest, Nahdlatul Ulama (NU), which was founded in East Java in 1926. NU is "traditionalist" in that it defends the incorporation of local ritual practices in religious life. These practices range from commemoration of the birthday of the Prophet and communal recitation of prayers to pilgrimages to the graves of respected religious teachers and other shrines. NU tends to follow the teachings of great ulama of the past rather than to focus on independent reasoning. In Java, NU's practices are reproduced through an educational system of *pesantren* (boarding schools) led by charismatic teachers (*kyai*), who place a strong emphasis on study of the classical Arabic texts and *fiqh*, the jurisprudence of one of the four Sunni schools of Islam. The critics of NU accuse it of "superstition, blind imitation of earlier generations, and beliefs and practices that are not supported by strong and authentic scriptural references," which sometimes include "relations with the spirit world, intercession by saints, and various forms of magic" (van Bruinessen 2013, 22).

In contrast to the traditionalism of NU is the "modernist" or "reformist" stream of Muhammadiyah, which was established in Yogyakarta in 1912. Muhammadiyah founder Ahmad Dahlan came from a prominent family; his father was a religious scholar affiliated with the Sultan's mosque. Frustrated with local religious practices, Ahmad Dahlan visited Mecca twice, first in 1890 and then again around 1902. It is believed that he learned about the ideas of the reformist Muhammed 'Abduh through the magazine *Al-Manar* (Menchik 2016, 38–39). Part of a global movement to modernize and purify Islam by purging it of practices not supported by the Qur'an and the Hadith, Muhammadiyah emphasizes scientific education and social reform. Its schools have a modern curriculum, no charismatic *kyai*, and no Arabic texts. Nahdlatul Ulama was founded by the traditionalists in direct response to the perceived threat to traditional religious practices that Muhammadiyah and the reformists seemed to pose.

More recently, during the Soeharto years, Indonesia has seen the rise of a new kind of Islamic movement outside of both Muhammadiyah and NU, the networks of "semiclandestine" Islamic study groups formed as part of the *tarbiyah* (Islamic education) movement that emerged on college campuses in the 1980s. One of these networks was the Indonesian branch of the Muslim Brotherhood, which later organized the political party Partai Keadilan (PK, Justice Party), the predecessor to the Prosperous Justice Party (Partai Keadilan Sejahtera, PKS) (van Bruinessen 2013, 29).[3] *Sabili* magazine, in its underground days, was associated with both the *tarbiyah* movement and the beginnings of the Justice Party. As anthropologist Martin van Bruinessen has noted, an important aspect differentiating the *tarbiyah* movement from both Muhammadiyah and NU is its transnational character. Whereas Muhammadiyah and NU "are national organizations, in the sense of . . . having been part of the movement for national independence and being dedicated to the idea of Indonesia as a nation," the *tarbiyah* movement was inspired by authorities outside of Indonesia and "owed allegiance to authorities based in the Middle East" (ibid., 30).

THE NEW ORDER

By the time *Sabili* was founded in 1984, Indonesian Muslims felt marginalized, despite being the numerical majority. In 1966 the army had depended on Nahdlatul Ulama and its youth wing Ansor to carry out the anti-Communist pogrom that took place in East Java, but Muslim leaders who were expecting to be rewarded for their loyalty were sorely disappointed (Hefner 2000). It quickly became clear that the New Order government had no intention of reviving the Jakarta Charter. Soeharto's refusal to allow for the return of the banned political party Masyumi (Majelis Syuro Muslimin Indonesia, or the Indonesian Muslim Consultative Council), as well as his 1973 forced "simplification" of the Muslim political parties into the government-approved grouping of the Development Unity Party (Partai Persatuan Pembangunan, PPP) only added to the feelings of anger and resentment.

The New Order's view of religion was that whereas religious activities should be encouraged and supported by the state, such activities should be altogether removed from the sphere of political parties and organizations. Islamic studies specialist Luthfi Assyaukani (2009, 103) explains that this model, which he has called "the religious democratic state," rests on two premises: the acceptance of Pancasila as the basis of the state, and the rejection of secularism. This model does two important things: it rejects the concept of the Islamic state and endorses the state's establishment of religion (ibid., 110). Religion is thus transformed into something private, outside of politics, and the struggle for the Islamic state is replaced with the goal of creating a religious society.

In 1971, Mukti Ali was chosen to be Soeharto's minister of religious affairs, "with the expectation that [he] would devote his expertise and concern to the reorientation of religious policy in Indonesia, which must go in the direction of the New Order's ideals of a religiopolitical strategy of modernization" (Munhanif 1996, 103). Although Mukti Ali was very much associated with the New Order strategy on religion, the difficulty lay in convincing Indonesian Muslims that the development policy of modernization was not at the same time a cultural strategy designed to secularize or separate religion from the state. Almost immediately Mukti Ali was attacked as a lackey of the Centre for Strategic and International Studies (CSIS), which was dominated by Catholics and adherents of Javanese spiritualism, and nowhere more vociferously than in the fight over the proposed 1974 Marriage Bill. Although the bill was intended to unify the national law on marriage for all Indonesians, many saw its provisions as a political plot to secularize Muslims.

PLOTS, CONSPIRACY, AND PARANOIA

Syamsul Rijal (2005, 425) of IAIN Makassar has noted that "a study of the resurgence of Islamism in post-Soeharto Indonesia would not be comprehensive without considering *Sabili*," and of the five media organizations examined in this book, *Sabili* is the only one that forthrightly embraces the term "Islamic." First established in 1984 as an underground paper, *Sabili* passed from hand to hand on college campuses and among members of *tarbiyah* groups, who became the magazine's most loyal readers. *Sabili*'s critical coverage of military excesses such as the 1984 Tanjung Priok incident (in which the Indonesian military opened fire on a group of unarmed Muslim protestors) caused the magazine and those allied with it to be stigmatized by the New Order as the "extreme right," which, along with the "extreme left" of Communism, was depicted as an existential threat to the regime (Irawanto 2011, 75). When *Sabili* shut itself down in response to a summons from Soeharto's security apparatus in 1993, it had a circulation of about sixty thousand.

Like *Tempo*, *Sabili* returned to publication in 1998 as the beneficiary of *reformasi*, and by 2002 it claimed a weekly readership of over four hundred

Sabili editor Eman Mulyatman with the author, 2013. Photo by author.

thousand, although this number is impossible to verify. It went out of business during the first week of April 2013, a development that most former *Sabili* writers attribute to bad financial management. Although the magazine was spawned by the same *tarbiyah* (Islamic education) movement that resulted in the formation of the Islamic party Partai Keadilan Sejahtera (PKS, the Prosperous Justice Party), *Sabili* was never formally affiliated with any political organization. This stands in stark contrast to *Harakah* in Malaysia, which is the organ of the country's Islamic party PAS (Parti Islam Se-Malaysia). Despite this lack of formal affiliation, former director Lutfi Tamimi estimates that in the years prior to its closing, up to 90 percent of *Sabili*'s editors and reporters were members of PKS.

Founded initially as a magazine focusing on *dakwah* (Islamic propagation), *Sabili*, upon its return to publication in 1998, was more concerned with political Islam, "typically from the viewpoint of hardliners," and support for the formal application of sharia (Rijal 2005, 427). When I interviewed *Sabili*'s final chief editor Eman Mulyatman in March 2013, he confirmed that the five main topics of the magazine were apostasy, Christianization, deviant sects, the "problem" of liberal Islam, and such international Islamic issues as the Israeli-Palestinian conflict. In truth, *Sabili* appeared obsessed with these topics, devoting page after page to the ways in which its enemies allegedly sought to undermine Islam. The perpetrators? Zionists, the West, and liberals, and *Sabili* carefully documented their methods. Although the enemies of Islam "sometimes dress like Muslims," there is no mistaking their agenda: "what they want to plant is feminism, secularism, pluralism, [and] liberalism." Their method is to "sow doubt, approach Allah from the perspective of logic, and chart a new course for Islam in the guise of moderation" (Satria and Handoko 2010). In this regard, *Sabili*'s preoccupations with the "global conspiracy against Islam" paralleled almost exactly those of the Muslim Brotherhood in Egypt. (Kandill 2015, 54–58).

A feature story on apostasy offered some specifics as to how missionaries encourage Christianization. These included providing food, financial, and emotional assistance to recent migrants to Jakarta, many of whom could only find work as scavengers. Victims of landslides and earthquakes along with the blind and other "marginal groups" likewise became the targets of missionaries. *Sabili* noted that children were especially vulnerable to the temptations of Christmas gifts, which might include books, toys, and money for scholarships. The magazine accused international NGOs (such as Doctors without Borders, Church World Services, World Vision, Oxfam, and Save the Children) and "Zionist groups" (such as the Rotary Club and the Lions) of trying to take advantage of disasters in order to weaken Islam and promote Christianization (Nurdi 2010). *Sabili* alerted its readers to some of the Christians' other "tricks," which included funding small businesses that needed capital or "marrying village girls who needed money for their weddings" and then "later" announcing that the children that appeared from these unions (especially the boys) were Christian and must be baptized. "This is something that is often done by Catholics," one of *Sabili*'s sources concluded (Satria 2010a).

As *Tempo* senior editor Idrus Shahab once noted: "When we talk about *Sabili*, it is opinion; [journalism] has to include data." It is true that the magazine contained a number of stories that couldn't really be considered journalism at all. For example, a cover story in January 2013 attributed severe flooding in Jakarta to a punishment from Allah for "car free night" and fireworks at the national monument on New Year's Eve. A feature in the back-of-the-book section pointed out that jeans and other "sexy and tight" clothing on women were not only the same as being naked but also the gateway to hell.[4] When I asked Eman Mulyatman whether he considered such articles to be journalism, he said: "Indeed, it is a problem of lack of study. There are also temptations when you work at *Sabili*. Maybe the temptation is to weaken your journalism. Maybe there is a temptation to direct yourself towards the mission of *dakwah*. I think this is the problem." He added:

> The problem of writing in *Sabili* is that from the very beginning it was not run by journalists. But the idea I try hard to convey is that if we use the weapons of media, we have to use the ethics of journalism—and journalism that is good. We have to use sources from both sides, and pay attention to the context. I always emphasize that we play in the field of journalistic *dakwah*. Therefore we have to follow the rules. When we play in a football field, then we have to follow the football rules. Don't play football in a badminton field! That's the mistake. I always emphasize that. But yes, maybe in practice there are friends who are too enthusiastic.

UNDERGROUND DAYS

According to Eman Mulyatman, from the very beginning, *Sabili* reporters not only had to have journalistic capability, they also had to side with Islam. All *Sabili* journalists were active in the Islamic movement, having either a background in Islamic student organizations such as Pelajar Islam Indonesia (PII) or the *tarbiyah* movement. Some graduated from Islamic institutes such as the Institute of Islamic and Arabic Sciences (Lembaga Ilmu Pengetahuan Islam dan Bahasa Arab, LIPIA), which was established in cooperation with the governments of Indonesia and the Kingdom of Saudi Arabia and known to promote Wahhabi Salafism (Alimah 2012, 64; Rijal 2005, 439).

During the magazine's first underground phase, between 1988 and 1993, *Sabili* was directly connected with the *tarbiyah* movement; one study referred to the magazine as the "voice of *tarbiyah*" (Pardini n.d.). The *tarbiyah* movement used small campus study groups, known as *usrah*, which were modeled after the system of cells used for caderization by the Muslim Brotherhood. One of the first and most famous of these study groups was found in the Salman Mosque at the Bandung Institute of Technology; its atmosphere was vividly described by the writer V. S. Naipaul in *Among the Believers* (1982, 361–79). Coauthors Anthony Bubalo and Greg Fealy (2005) have noted that although *tarbiyah* members regarded Islam and the state as "inseparable," they did not see the creation of the Islamic state as immediately possible or even necessary. "Echoing al-Banna's approach, Islamisation of the state was seen as a gradual process that must begin with greater pietism within society" (ibid. 2005, 68).

The original idea for *Sabili*, which means "my path" in Arabic, came from a group of five young *tarbiyah* activists who believed that a magazine would help spread their revivalist campaign. One of these was Zainal Muttaqin, who became the first editor of *Sabili*.

When Zainal Muttaqin, described by Eman Mulyatman as "the Goenawan Mohamad of *Sabili*," became the magazine's founding editor, he was a young journalist with experience writing for Islamic media. Born in Banten, West Java, Zainal Muttaqin came from a family that was "thick in *dakwah*," with Masyumi figures on one side and a founder of the Islamic organization Mathla'ul Anwar on the other. With very little capital, he managed to turn what started out as a half-folio-sized bimonthly with irregular wages and a sporadic publishing schedule into a professionally run magazine.

According to Zainal, since the beginning, the problem with *Sabili* was not the market but rather how to establish "quality control," which was the biggest challenge facing Islamic media: "It's like this [with other Islamic media]. Imagine there is an important *kyai*, a big man who writes something, certainly he will be included. Suppose an editor writes something, then he goes home, certainly it will be included. At *Sabili*, it will not. Everyone who writes, including me, the chief editor, has to be tested by the team. Checked. Checked and rechecked! If it's not good, it's out. If we try to do our best, then Allah will make people appreciate us." During its underground phase, *Sabili* aspired to be "intelligent, of high quality, and professional." The idea was that a magazine could help spread positive revivalist thinking, while at the same time counter negative images of Islam that grew out of Western media (Pardini n.d.). Because the *tarbiyah* movement was based on self-study, the *usrah* (study groups) needed appropriate teaching materials, and one of *Sabili*'s goals was to fill that gap.

Under President Soeharto's New Order government, Indonesia's press was tightly controlled through a series of regulations enacted and enforced by the Ministry of Information. One of the first pieces of legislation passed by the New Order government was the Basic Press Act of 1966. Although the law explicitly stated that "freedom of the press is guaranteed in accordance with the fundamental rights of citizens," this was not the case (Hill 1994, 25). Despite guarantees that there would be no censorship or press bannings, would-be press entrepreneurs were required to obtain two permits before they could publish a newspaper or magazine: the Permit to Publish (Surat Izin Terbit, SIT) from the Department of Information and the Permit to Print (Surat Izin Cetak, SIC) from the military security authority (Kopkamtib).[5] A newspaper could be effectively banned by the withdrawal of either one.

As an underground publication, *Sabili* did not have either a permit to publish or a permit to print. Its directors used assumed names, and the magazine—which by 1993 claimed to have a circulation of sixty thousand— had no office and paid no taxes. According to Zainal, all of the writers were young people, mostly under age twenty-five, and students. Zainal himself was still in his twenties. "Bakin" (Indonesian intelligence) was "certain that there must have been a big person behind it," he said, laughing. "These must be big people, great people, intellectuals!"

According to writer Agung Pardini, who had the opportunity to review about half of the existing seventy or so copies of the magazine, aside from *dakwah*, the main focus of *Sabili* was the "Islamic World," in which reports focused on the Islamic struggle in Afghanistan, Bosnia, and Palestine. Most of these stories came directly from overseas contributors or the Islamic press in the Middle East and Pakistan. "In the era of Soeharto," Zainal said, "it was not possible to speak directly. We would have been detained. So we used the language of insinuation . . . the news was more from overseas, from Patani, from Myanmar." He said: "After Soeharto, we reversed. During the euphoria, we had lots of news [of Indonesia]. If we wrote like that during the Soeharto era, we would have certainly been detained." Zainal Muttaqin is not the first Indonesian editor to have noted that under the restrictions of Soeharto's New Order government, it was generally best to comment obliquely about Indonesia while seeming to focus on an entirely different country (Steele 2005).

It is interesting to assess why the government didn't close down *Sabili*. Again, Agung Pardini (n.d.) suggests three explanations: the Soeharto regime was in an "accommodative phase" toward Islam, which was seen as a check on the pro-democracy movement; the Soeharto regime was trying to curry favor with the Islamic community; and *Sabili*, by focusing as it did on international rather than domestic politics, was not seen as a threat. In the late 1980s many observers noted the growing power of elements of the Indonesian military that were allied with Catholic General Benny Murdani and understood Soeharto's overtures toward Islam, including his 1990 Hajj pilgrimage, as an attempt at maintaining balance (Hefner 1993, 24; Crouch 1988). Soeharto's pivot toward Islam was in all likelihood the result of these factors plus recognition of the rapidly growing Muslim middle class—something that led to both the 1991 establishment of ICMI, the Association of Indonesian Muslim Intellectuals, and the founding of *Republika* newspaper (Hefner 1993; Hefner 1997b).

Despite these developments, in 1993 the security apparatus decided to clamp down on *Sabili*. In December 1992 a letter to the editor told of a woman wearing hijab who was harassed by Christian missionaries who forced her at knifepoint "to give up all her jewelry and to say Christian words" (Rijal 2005, 434). The letter was seen to violate the SARA law, an acronym for a set of guidelines prohibiting the reporting of anything that might inflame ethnic, religious, racial, or group (class) tensions. Although the editors' names were concealed, the magazine used a post office box for correspondence, and *Sabili*'s editor-in-chief received a summons from the Jakarta High Court. Aware that the summons was in reality a plan to arrest him, Zainal decided instead to close down the magazine.

After Soeharto was forced to step down, *Sabili* roared back to print. Zainal found new investors, Muslim businessmen who wanted to own shares in the new company. The biggest shareholder was Rahmat Ismail, who also owned *Forum* magazine. Zainal himself owned 10 percent of the shares. The market was there: the first print run in 1999 was twenty-five thousand copies (Muhammad 2001). A. Mabruri M. Akbari, the general manager of several Islamist magazines, noted that in this way *Sabili* was like *Tempo*: the magazine could be banned but not its readers. "When *Sabili* was banned in 1993, it left behind many readers. When it returned to publication in 1998, with banners everywhere, people were curious, especially the loyal readership that was pretty big before," he said (quoted in Muhammad 2001, 6).

Sabili journalists were hired because they were strong in *dakwah*. Many of them came from secular universities, which are known to attract more Islamist students (Rijal 2005, 439). Eman Mulyatman explained that when *Sabili* journalists are in the field, they are seen as *ustad* (Islamic scholars and teachers). "When we go out to the regions to report, they don't see us as journalists. Sometimes during the conversation we are even invited to give a sermon." As I was told by members of the *dakwah* faculties at several Indonesian Islamic universities and institutes—where journalism and communication studies are generally located—one of the goals of Islamic journalism is to be inspiring or even "prophetic" (Steele 2012). In 2013, Eman Mulyatman said something similar of *Sabili*: "*Sabili* has to become an *inspirator* for the *umat* Islam. Now this is the change I want: *Sabili* has to become an *inspirator*."

The fact that *Sabili* journalists were strong in *dakwah* but weak in journalism is clear from even a quick perusal of the magazine. Even editors of other Islamic magazines noted that the style of *Sabili* was "distorted," "bombastic," "excessive," and too quick to label an issue very important, "as if it threatened the Muslim community" (quoted in Muhammad 2001, 6). For example, a story entitled "Atheist Intrigue: Beware: Communism Is Rising Again," cited "research" about the "national phenomenon" of the rise of atheism in the United States—which the magazine then connected with Communism, the alleged resurgence of the Indonesian Communist Party, attempts by liberals to twist Indonesian history, and efforts by atheists to overturn the Indonesian law that criminalized blasphemy. It was not only Christians who attempted to undermine Islam, *Sabili* warned, but also atheists disguised as Communists (Satria 2010b).

It is worth noting that a perceived connection between the eradication of the Indonesian Communist Party (Partai Komunis Indonesia, PKI) and adherence to Islam has existed in Indonesia since the mass killings of 1965–66, a pogrom that was unleashed by General Soeharto in response to the alleged coup attempt of G30S, the Thirtieth of September Movement of 1965. As political scientist Jeremy Menchik (2016) has painstakingly documented, Nahdlatul Ulama (NU) and its subsidiary body Ansor provided anti-PKI hit squads that, in coordination with the military, conducted systematic killings of Communists, suspected Communists, and Communist sympathizers. NU *kyai* also provided "moral sanction" through fatwas declaring that the "PKI were unbelievers who were belligerent toward Islam (*kafir harbi*), and rebels against a legitimate government (*bughat*)" (ibid., 117). This sentiment, matched by declarations from Muhammadiyah, "fused the idea that eradicating Communists was an act of adherence to Islamic law" and made "the duties of national citizenship . . . synonymous with those of faith" (ibid., 121).

In 2001, Atmakusumah Astraatmadja, the head of the Indonesian Press Council, described *Sabili* as a "pamphlet." These words stung, and then-editor Herry Nurdi invited the senior press observer to visit the magazine for a dialogue. Atmakusumah remained firm in his convictions, pointing out that although *Sabili* had a right to express its views, its reports weren't in keeping with either journalistic ethics or standards. Journalists have to work hard to be accurate, fair, and not take sides, he said. "If A accuses B, the voice of B has to be heard also" (quoted in Muhammad 2001).

The biases found in *Sabili* have inspired countless Indonesian master's theses, undergraduate *skripsi*, and even a few doctoral dissertations (Chusjairi 2014; Alimah 2012). media scholar Juni Alfiah Chusjairi, for example, analyzed *Sabili*'s coverage of the Bali, Marriot, and Australian embassy bombings, comparing it with that of other more mainstream magazines including *Tempo*. She found that whereas 41 percent of *Tempo*'s sources cited were either police or government officials, these types of individuals accounted for only 23 percent of *Sabili*'s sources. Another 29 percent of the sources cited by *Sabili* came from Islamist organizations, nearly all of whom supported the notion that it was not Jama'ah Islamiyah that was behind the bombings, but rather "the West" (Chusjairi 2014, 95). Of the thirty possible news frames in the *Sabili* stories Chusjairi examined, nearly half drew upon the idea that the bombings were a conspiracy to "undermine and stigmatize Islam" (ibid., 98). Related to this were other common themes of "the Western agenda" to extend its hegemony and weaken Indonesia as well as the claim that the bomb materials must have come from Western countries, as these materials were "hard to find in Indonesia" (ibid., 99).

If Chusjairi's research addressed what was widely believed to be *Sabili*'s anti-Western perspective, then Alimah's work (2012) demonstrated the magazine's obsession with heterodox sects within Islam, especially Ahmadiyah. As Menchik (2016, 72) has argued, Indonesia is not a liberal democratic state but instead "contains a form of nationalism that is neither Islamic nor secular, but rather exclusively and assertively religious." Calling this "godly nationalism" and arguing that it occupies a "middle position" between religious and secular nationalism, Menchik (ibid., 72) suggests that although godly nationalism is plural and "promotes belief in God through multiple religions," it is at the same time predicated on theological exclusion and denies "liminal groups, heterodox groups, and non-believers" the full benefits of citizenship. Ahmadis, believing as they do that Mirza Ghulam Ahmad, the movement's founder, was the final prophet or "renewer" of Islam, are sufficiently heterodox to be considered "deviant" or "non-Muslim" by Indonesia's three largest Islamic organizations (ibid., 73).

Noting that editions of *Sabili* that contained stories about deviant sects always sold well, Alimah (2012, 66) found 103 stories about Ahmadiyah published between 2000 and 2013. These were usually bundled into packages consisting of the headline story, interviews, and opinion—all of which were mutually reinforcing. Given that each of these types of articles presented exactly the same data and quoted the same sources, Alimah (ibid., 105) concluded that when it came to the Ahmadiyah, it was difficult to distinguish between news and opinion. In reporting on Ahmadiyah, *Sabili*'s primary reference was the Indonesian Council of Ulama (Majelis Ulama Indonesia, MUI) fatwa of 2005, which declared Ahmadiyah to be heretical. The fatwa is widely believed to have spawned attacks on Indonesia's Ahmadiyah community, some of them deadly. *Sabili* editor Eman Mulyatman told Alimah it was logical that the MUI fatwa became the frame of reference, in that it was the most authoritative on the topic (ibid., 67–68).

Sabili may have been simply reporting on the fatwas of others, but its decisions carried weight. "Whatever *Sabili* writes, others follow," Eman said (quoted in ibid., 69). In many instances, *Sabili*'s critique of Ahmadiyah bled over into its criticism of the Liberal Islamic Network and its most famous member, Ulil Abshar Abdalla. Although many Muslims defended Ahmadiyah as a minority group with the right to be free from harassment and physical attacks, only Jaringan Islam Liberal (JIL, Liberal Islamic Network) defended its right to exist as a group within Islam. As Ulil said, he was "fighting not only for their right to exist but also to be recognized as part of Islam."[6]

Sabili's perspective was clear: Islam and the Muslim community were under siege from a variety of enemies, including Christians, Western governments such as the United States, "Orientalists," and those who would argue that all religions are basically the same. As Eman Mulyatman said, "Pluralism yes, we accept it as the reality. But if all religions are seen as right and true, then that is the view we oppose." The position outlined by Eman Mulyatman is essentially that of the "godly nationalism" described by Menchik (2016). The 1965 "blasphemy law" (Presidential Order No. 1/1965) formalized an orthodox definition of religion by prohibiting "telling, encouraging, or soliciting public support for making an interpretation of a religion adhered to in Indonesia or performing religious activities resembling the activities of such religion when the interpretation and activities are deviant from the principal teachings of such religion" (quoted in Menchik 2016, 79).

This law, which was upheld by the Constitutional Court in 2009, means that anyone practicing a religion outside the orthodox definition is not entitled to either protection or resources from the state. Defenders of the law, which include MUI and the Ministry of Religious Affairs, argue that the Ahmadis' constitutional right to freedom of religion is not being violated because they are "permitted their internal beliefs." Any public expressions of faith are a different matter and can be restricted, as the state is "obligated to prohibit the dissemination of deviant religious beliefs in order to promote belief in God" (ibid., 85). As Menchik concludes, by "promoting belief in God, maintaining the state's religious identity while respecting pluralism, distinguishing internal freedom from external freedom, combating deviant beliefs through law rather than violence, and protecting the dignity of religion," the government uses "a vocabulary imbued with commitments to pluralism," which is nevertheless entirely different from that of the liberal, secular West (ibid., 90).

Given its focus on orthodoxy, it is not surprising that for *Sabili* the greatest threat to Islam came from those who were already within the gates: liberal Muslims. In this regard, *Sabili* resembled the "counter-cosmopolitans" described by philosopher Kwame Anthony Appiah (2006). Although the magazine shared with other cosmopolitans a commitment to a transnational ideology and a global community (in *Sabili*'s case, the *umat*), it rejected "as a sham [much of] what passes for Islam in the world" (ibid., 138). Like the "neofundamentalists" described by political scientist Olivier Roy (2004, 155), *Sabili* claimed to be upholding the "pristine" message of Islam that is threatened by "foreigners or 'bad' Muslims." *Sabili* shared with the cosmopolitans a quest for universal truths, but in its certainty of the truth of its own convictions, the magazine lacked both the cosmopolitan "realism about how hard the truth is to find" and "the sense that our knowledge is imperfect, provisional, [and] subject to revision in the face of new evidence" (Appiah 2006, 144).

JIL, *Tempo* founding editor Goenawan Mohamad, and the Utan Kayu and Salihara arts and cultural communities thus became targets of the magazine's vitriol, and *Sabili* popularized a clever and insulting term for what it considered to be the three most dangerous elements of liberal Islam: *sepilis* (secularism, liberalism, and pluralism) (Satria 2009, 44; Ruspiyandi 2013, 40). According to *Sabili*, liberals drew in young people with comfortable, "home-like" places such as Goenawan Mohamad's Salihara community, tempting them with attractive architecture and facilities, coffee and tea, and Wi-Fi hotspots: "So that the virus of liberalism won't inflame the body of Islamic mass organizations, the most effective step is to check it now. If it has already spread, then a vaccine must be developed to sterilize and shake loose the virus from where it has lodged. To stop the spread of liberalism, Islamic organizations can't be passive. They have to prepare the best cadres possible to scrape away this deviant understanding" (Satria 2009, 47).

"It can be imagined," *Sabili* concluded, "how powerful the cadreization of these liberals is. Islamic mass organizations cannot remain quiet. The time has arrived for the birth of activists that will defend the Islamic faith and attack liberalism, because Islamic organizations like Muhammadiyah and NU are the two biggest in the homeland. Like a fish, if the head rots, then the entire thing will rot. Don't let that happen" (Nasrul 2009, 42).

Sabili blamed the spreading infection of *sepilis* not only on young intellectuals who had received secular educations abroad but also on Indonesian campus study groups, such as the Ciputat Student Forum (Forum Mahasiswa Ciputat, Formaci) at the Syarif Hidayatullah State Islamic University in Jakarta. *Sabili* accused Formaci of supporting secularization, refusing the implementation of sharia, endorsing marriage among those of different religions, and ignoring the command to invite good and prohibit evil. In May 2002, referring to the university's previous name (IAIN Syarif Hidayatullah Jakarta), *Sabili*'s cover featured a photo of the main university building with the headline "IAIN: Ingkar Allah, Ingkar Nabi" (IAIN renounces God, renounces the Prophet).[7] Azyumardi Azra, the university's highly regarded rector, went to see Rahmat Ismail, one of *Sabili*'s owners, and asked if the magazine had intended to call him an apostate. According to Azyumardi Azra, "Rahmat apologized and asked for forgiveness." Azyumardi recalls saying in response, "Restrain yourself from making smear campaigns."

As these examples and many others suggest, *Sabili* wasn't balanced at all. How did the editors justify this? Eman Mulyatman said that he thought that other media did the same thing. "They take sides," he said. "*Tempo* takes sides. *Sabili* certainly has a mission. Our vision and mission; it is our editorial policy. But in the process, I always emphasize you have to use the rules of journalism." Although many would disagree with Eman's argument that because *Tempo* was "unbalanced" *Sabili* should be too, he does make an important point. As former *Malaysiakini* journalist Fauwaz Abdul Aziz pointed out in an article called "The Secularists' Crusade," often liberals do not see their own values as an ideology. Quoting Australian National University professor Michael Wesley, Fauwaz noted: "Secularism has itself become a messianic religion, convinced of its own infallibility, hostile towards dissent, and determined to place strict limits on how all other systems of faith and belief in society are practiced."[8] In this regard, Fauwaz (and Wesley) support what sociologist Herbert Gans observed many years ago in American newsrooms: journalists tend to identify "ideology" only as those political values at the extreme ends of the political spectrum. As Gans (1979, 192) concluded, "the journalists' definition of ideology is self-serving, if not intentionally so, for it blinds them to the fact that they also have ideologies, even if these are largely unconscious."

When Indonesian journalists refer to balanced stories, they use the word *seimbang*. As in English, a synonym for balance in news is "fair," which Indonesians translate as *adil*, or just. Sociologist Gaye Tuchman (1972) has shown that the presentation of conflicting possibilities, or "covering both sides," is one of the components of what American journalists mean when they say that a story is "objective." Zainal Muttaqin, the founding editor of *Sabili*, said that the claim of the mainstream press (media like *Tempo*)—that they were covering both sides—was "nonsense": "We think the press is very unjust: Why? Because it only gives space to certain people. Here's an example. In Indonesia, if they need an expert on Islam, the person they interview is Nurcholish Madjid or Abdurahman Wahid. As if there are no other Islamic figures! There are many Islamic figures. But when they interview one, it is always Cak Nur or Gus Dur. This is another example of ideology, and also a kind of injustice."

Former *Sabili* editor Herry Nurdi has wrestled with the criticism that his magazine is not balanced. "When Pak Atma [of the Dr. Soetomo Press Institute] says that *Sabili* isn't balanced, that it's conservative and puritan, we truly think about what we should do," he said. "We aren't angry, we truly consider it." Although Herry said that he sees the values of Islam and the values of journalism as complementary, especially in the realms of verification and covering both sides, most neutral observers would agree with the criticism that *Sabili* is not balanced. When presented with this critique, Herry said: "Now, most media, they don't have any sources other than the police when they are covering the issue of terrorism. So they aren't balanced. For example, if *Tempo* does an independent investigation, all of its information comes from Detachment 88 [the special Indonesian police unit assigned to investigate terrorism]. So *Sabili* plays the role of dissenting opinion. What isn't said by the police, or by other sources, we will say. Now ideally, it shouldn't be like that. *Sabili* can't play that role forever. It should be in the center, choosing facts. But there has to be balance."

Herry Nurdi is famous, but his fame is a mixed blessing. The "fanatic" of Sadanand Dhume's *My Friend the Fanatic* (2009), Herry was always well known as the editor of *Sabili* and considered to be something of an *ustad* himself, but now he's notorious. Some people think he must be a spy; for why else would he have agreed to take Dhume, a nonbeliever, to meet key Islamist players like Abu Bakar Ba'asyir in the first place? Others are angry, wondering why he was so open with a writer whose plan seemed to be to ridicule much of what he holds dear.

I have known Herry since 2004; in fact, it was Sadanand Dhume who first introduced us. To everyone's surprise, Herry and I liked one another. I saw him as a smart, self-educated young man who seemed much like the other earnest young journalists I had met at places like Yayasan Pantau, where I often taught. I was working on my own book on *Tempo* at the time and was impressed with Herry's searching questions. "How can you write objectively about *Tempo* when you are such an admirer of Goenawan's?" he asked. It was a fair question. As time went by, Herry and I became friends. When he visited Washington, DC, on the US government–sponsored International Visitor's program, I met him there. We had lemonade in a café near the Newseum, and Herry saw his first snowfall. Later I helped him buy a cheap netbook so that he could take advantage of free Wi-Fi to stay in touch with his wife and family. My view of him has never really changed from the time I first met him: Herry is bright, entirely self-educated, and an opportunist. The first people ever to have paid attention to him or to take him seriously were the Islamists. It could easily have been different.

Herry is from a Nahdlatul Ulama (NU) family in Surabaya and grew up in the Kampung Mesjid Sunan Ampel, named after one of the nine *wali songo* ("saints") who brought Islam to Indonesia in the fifteenth century. Many of its residents are of Arab descent, and Herry explains that his grandmother was an Arab who married a man from Madura. His mother is illiterate, but she wanted Herry to go to school. "Don't be like me, she said." Herry studied at the Pesantren Hidayatullah, which is conservative if not as

Former *Sabili* editor Herry Nurdi, 2016. Photo by author.

traditionalist as Nahdlatul Ulama or as reformist as Muhammadiyah. Known for its connections to the Darul Islam movement, Hidayatullah has been described as reflecting "a very Indonesian approach to Islam" while at the same time supporting the "*jihad* of oppressed Muslims" everywhere (van Bruinessen 2015, 75).

"My own family is an NU family, but my own religious behavior is more like Muhammadiyah," Herry said. "For example, how I wear my *sarong* above my feet. My grandmother says don't wear your *sarong* like Muhammadiyah! When I was little I felt the conflict between NU and Muhammadiyah in my *kampung* . . . sometimes it even became a physical conflict. So it made me think why is it like this? We are brothers." When I asked Herry where he fits on the map of Islam in Indonesia, he said: "I am an Indonesian Muslim. There is only Islam, moderate Islam and others. And I struggle for what's moderate. And the others, there is radical and there is liberal. For me, there is a problem with the word 'moderate,' because it has been hijacked by the West, liberals hijacked the word 'moderate' to make it become the new liberal."

Although Herry did not attend university, he is probably unique among *Sabili* journalists for having completed an intensive journalism training program at the Dr. Soetomo Press Institute. Two of his teachers were Amir Daud, formerly of *Tempo*, and Atmakusumah, formerly of Mochtar Lubis's *Indonesia Raya*. "Pak Amir was so strict!" Herry said. "I learned so much about how Muslim journalists have to do tight verification, choose good words, and have a clean perspective." Herry was almost entirely self-trained as a journalist, but he could immediately see the applications of what he learned to Islam. "LPDS gave me technical skills to complete what I already knew about Islam," he added. "Because there was no *ustad* who could teach me about the theory of journalism."

Although it was not always apparent in their stories, each of the three *Sabili* editors whom I met had a well-thought-out philosophy of journalism. For Herry, part of this was being seen as "alternative media." He said: "People say *Sabili* has its own *mazhab* [school of thought], but not really because in terms of *fikh*, we are Sunni." He argued that when *Sabili* came back to publication in 1998, it was as an alternative. "We emerged during the Ambon conflict," he said, referring to the violence between Christians and Muslims in Maluku that began at the start of the *reformasi* era. "And at that time there were not many media that were giving facts about the Ambon conflict. So we became alternative media." At that time, he added, *Sabili* was more concerned with politics than religion. "When I became the managing editor in 2002," he said, "I wanted to make *Sabili* a dissenting opinion, another voice."

Although *Sabili* was never a proponent of the Islamic state, it nevertheless gave steadfast support to the view that sharia was the solution to Indonesia's problems. In this regard, it resembled other Salafist movements (Bubalo and Fealy 2005, 39). As Islamic studies specialist Syamsul Rijal (2005) has noted, in Indonesia there are two common discourses for implementing sharia: one is the formal establishment of an Islamic state, and the other is a return to the Jakarta Charter, with the insertion of the words "with the obligation of the adherents of Islam to carry out sharia" into the constitution. *Sabili* was far more likely to suggest the second than the first (ibid., 449). *Sabili*'s arguments in favor of sharia were varied but hinged largely on the fact that secular-positive law has not worked in Indonesia and has led to corruption and widespread immorality among public officials. In this regard, *Sabili*'s critique is quite similar to that of Malaysia's *Harakah*. Other reasons included the idea that Indonesia is a majority Muslim society, resembling Madinah in the days of the Prophet. *Sabili* routinely put forth the argument that in Madinah, "Islamic values were able to bring justice to the various components of the society without discrimination in terms of religion, blood, or tribe" (ibid., 451).

When I asked Herry Nurdi in 2011 about his own view of the Islamic state, he surprised me by asking, "Is Indonesia an infidel country or an Islamic country?" Answering his own question, he said, "It is neither. And this is important because in Islam there is a terminology that says that we cannot live in an infidel country, except if we make changes. Now, those changes can be of many kinds, from structural changes to violence." He added: "So I think that Indonesia isn't either an infidel nation or an Islamic one. It is a Pancasila nation, until now and maybe into the future." He continued:

> If you read Pancasila, you see the first *sila* is belief in God. If you read the word *beradab* [civilized], it doesn't come from Sanskrit, from Dutch, or from the Malay language. It comes from Arabic. Before that, before the word entered Indonesia, there was no word for "civilized." And *keadilan*, justice, the fifth *sila*—in Indonesian, in Malay, in Sanskrit, there was no *adil*. They had no concept of justice. Therefore, even though the Jakarta Charter has not yet happened, the biggest ideas of Islam about *tawhid* [the oneness of God], about justice, and about being civilized had already entered. And for me, these three ideas are very big.
>
> In the ideal state, there is the category of sharia in an Islamic state with Islamic leaders. There is also sharia in an Islamic state with leaders that are not Islamic. And there can be sharia in a *kafir* state with *kafir* leaders and Muslim people. Muslims always have the alternative to implement sharia in their lives. . . . I think it can no longer be black or white, that you have to be completely an Islamic state or not.

THE END OF *SABILI*

Why did *Sabili* go out of business? The obvious answers are financial misman-agement and lack of advertising. When circulation was high, it didn't matter that *Sabili* had always found it difficult to attract advertisers (Muhammad 2001), but when circulation started to fall, trouble began. Although there were persistent rumors of outside funding for the magazine, former *Sabili* personnel are unanimous in their insistence that this was not the case. Yet this did not mean that outside money had not been involved. One of the clearest examples of outside funding was a gift from Muammar Gaddafi to

Lutfi Tamimi, one of the directors and shareholders of *Sabili*. What was this money for? Influence, probably. According to Lutfi Tamimi, Gaddafi was interested in stemming the influence of the Saudis in Indonesia—especially the Wahhabis—and gave Lutfi money to "support his fight."

There were two big turning points in the history of *Sabili*, and both seem to have been related to money. The first was the firing of Zainal Muttaqin in 2001, and the second was a 2009 anti-Salafi cover story that was published when editor Herry Nurdi was away on the Hajj. Although the details of both incidents are cloudy, they are nevertheless indicative of the atmosphere of intrigue and occasional skullduggery that operated behind the doors of the magazine. In March 2001, Zainal Muttaqin was "deactivated" as the chief editor of *Sabili*. In 2001 he would not explain to a *Pantau* reporter why this had occurred other than to say, "This is the risk we take in a capitalist system; those with power are those who have money" (as quoted in Muhammad 2001). Several years later he was not much more forthcoming, saying only that he had been an activist, "but they were business people."

The conflict seemed to focus on a difference of opinion between Zainal and Rahmat Ismail, who held the largest number of shares of *Sabili*. "Rahmat was a businessman," Zainal said in 2012. "He didn't have a vision. For me it was clear that *Sabili* had to be independent, defend truth and justice. For Rahmat, maybe business or politics was first." This is what led to conflict:

Obviously Rahmat had two kinds of business: one with Saudi people, and two with Libyans. At the time there was an article in *Sabili* that made an enemy of the Saudis. Rahmat pulled it. I said, this is an Islamic magazine, it is independent, it is not owned by the Saudis. So Rahmat was very mad at me because *Sabili* criticized the kingdom of Saudi. [Another time], Muammar Gaddafi killed some *ulama*, we exposed it! It made Rahmat mad. I said you are in business with Libya, business with the Saudis. This is your business. Don't involve *Sabili*. Our media is independent. You have to know, you can be rich, you can have money, but the contents have to be professional. As long as I am in charge, don't intervene.

According to Zainal, it was this same desire for independence from any particular group that had caused *Sabili* not to be affiliated with the Prosperous Justice Party (Partai Keadilan Sejahtera, PKS). Even though the magazine was "born as a child of *tarbiyah*," Zainal said that *Sabili* "is owned by the *umat* . . . all the people!" Concluding that under Rahmat "looking for money" became more important than the struggle, Zainal said, "I told our friends, our motto is 'Profit may come and go, what is important is *dakwah*.' *Dakwah* is our essence. If we make a profit, *Alhamdulilah*! If not, no matter."

Perhaps not surprisingly, Lutfi Tamimi's recollections of the ousting of Zainal are different, if equally murky. Lutfi seems to enjoy controversy, which sticks to him easily. Born in Pekalongan, he is of Arab descent; he has a thick black moustache and a flair for the dramatic. A businessman now, Lufti spent eighteen years in Saudi Arabia, working in security for the US embassy. His account of the firing of Zainal is full of intrigue, offers from politicians, secret promises of a government office in exchange for influence, and dark insinuations of an attempt by Zainal to set up a new, rival magazine. There are rumors of American influence—the CIA, even—and Indonesian intelligence plants among the shareholders. With Lutfi Tamimi, the bottom line is that everyone wants to capture *Sabili*, or at least claim that they can influence it. Fifteen years after the firing of Zainal Muttaqin, no one from *Sabili* is talking, and it is nearly impossible to determine what really happened.

The second crisis in *Sabili*'s history came to a head when then–chief editor Herry Nurdi went on the Hajj, and Lutfi saw to it that the magazine's cover story was "Gelombang Penolakan Salafi Extreme" ("A wave of rejecting Salafi extremism"). Lutfi is proud of this story, as he brought a bound copy of the magazine to our meeting in 2014. "You can have this," he said. Lutfi calls the war against the Salafis "the true fight," adding, "here I am alone." He said: "I know what is going on. They are very bad people. The money comes from Saudi Arabia, they make *yayasans* [foundations]; they make everything." Lutfi says he is afraid that one day Indonesia will shatter. "This is when I began my war with Wahhabis," he said dramatically. On the desk in front of us is a keychain that says "US Department of Defense."

"You can buy those anywhere," Herry Nurdi scoffs, dismissing the keychain as insignificant. Herry, while insisting that he will not discuss names, agrees that the attack on the Salafis was the final turning point and the beginning of the end. Although there are several versions of how the anti-Salafi story came to be published and why, it is clear that there was a breach of protocol when so controversial a story appeared while the magazine's chief editor was out of the country. Worse yet, Herry said, "All of the people who were there with me thought that I had done it."

Herry, who is reluctant to talk about this incident, says that although there had been pressure from some of the shareholders to attack the Salafis, he had never agreed, "because according to me this is attacking *umat* Islam." He said he called to protest, but it was too late. Although the edition became a top seller, Herry was concerned that both *Sabili* and he personally would be seen as shattering the Islamic community, "which is forbidden." "So slowly I stepped back," he said. "I became the editor of *Sabili Online*, I began publishing, and finally Lutfi asked me to leave." One reason that Herry Nurdi is unwilling to talk about what happened during the final year of *Sabili* is Islamic: his desire not to *"membuka aib"* (to bring shame upon someone else). *Ghibah*, or backbiting, is the intentional spreading of something detestable about another person. Not quite gossip, it is different from *fitnah* (libel) in that what you are repeating is true. The Qur'an makes this a profound sin.

It is possible that outsiders will never know what really happened at *Sabili*. There was considerable intrigue inside the magazine, including rumors that various shareholders and other *Sabili* personnel were "BIN" (Indonesian intelligence), "close to Golkar," "close to PDIP," or even CIA plants. There were stories of the directors trying to influence the editorial section and of outsiders trying to buy influence. "Everything was fighting over influence," Herry Nurdi said. Each of the former editors, reporters, and directors with whom I spoke agreed with this assessment. It was almost a source of pride that the magazine was perceived to be so important within Indonesian's Muslim community that everybody wanted to control it. With a weak management structure and an obvious market for influence peddling, the situation was combustible.

Might *Sabili* have survived longer had it been affiliated directly with the Prosperous Justice Party (Partai Keadilan Sejahtera, PKS)? According to Herry, the problem with such an affiliation would be not only that the magazine could no longer represent the entire *umat*, but that it would also run the risk of enjoying the struggle too much. "A year ago I was invited to Malaysia to speak to PAS, and I gave them the perspective that our duty as Muslims was to struggle. Not to enjoy the struggle. And if today PAS or PKS have begun to enjoy the struggle, this is wrong. Later you will forget the struggle." Yet what Herry sees as "enjoying the struggle" may also be interpreted as participating in the normal give-and-take of politics. Political scientists who study the "inclusion/moderation" thesis and the behavior of Islamist political parties have argued that in many cases parties that have "embraced the procedural dimension of democracy" and "participated in competitive elections" will moderate their views (Tomsa 2012, 487).

This process of moderation occurred not only with the Muslim Brotherhood in Egypt (Wickham 2013) but also with Turkey's Justice and Development party. Political scientist Julie Chernov Hwang (2010, 672) has demonstrated how Indonesia's Prosperous Justice Party and Malaysia's Islamist party PAS have both moderated their strategies, albeit for different reasons. If we consider the inclusion/moderation thesis in the realm of journalism, it is possible to explain at least in part why *Sabili* went out of business. *Sabili* was never formally affiliated with PKS, so the former *tarbiyah* activists who made up 90 percent of the journalists were never forced to take a more pragmatic stance in the same way that journalists writing for *Harakah* were. True to its scripturalist ideology to the end, *Sabili* was both unable and unwilling to change.

An editor at *Republika* once commented that whereas for journalists at his paper the world is a happy place, at *Sabili* it is frightening, marked by paranoia. *Tempo*'s chief editor Arif Zulkifli observed that this kind of suspicion was also typical of the campus *dakwah* movement; that "we were seen as lambs that needed to stay close to the flock, and away from the dangers of Christians, Jews, and others." Throughout its history, *Sabili* was characterized by paranoia—paranoia about Christianization, the power of Jews, American efforts to weaken or undermine Islam, and secret funding from the CIA or Indonesian intelligence. In this way *Sabili* reflected the agenda of the politically conservative movement that sustained it. Although the magazine is now long gone, there are plenty of other materials available that keep its version of political Islam alive.

TWO

REPUBLIKA

Islam as Market Niche

IT IS Christmas Day 2012, and I'm in a Blue Bird taxi on my way to Indonesia's *Republika* newspaper for the daily editorial meeting. "O Come All Ye Faithful" is playing on the radio, but Kasno, the Javanese driver, turns it off as we enter Jalan (Jl.) Rasuna Said, a major artery heading south. The roads are empty, and I'm going to *Republika* because I want to see how the journalists there will interact with me on Christmas. I am especially curious about whether they will say "Selamat Natal," which more or less translates as "Merry Christmas." This year, as always, there has been some controversy about these words, with many Muslims electing to follow the Council of Indonesian Ulama (Majelis Ulama Indonesia, MUI) fatwa suggesting that Muslims should not extend Christmas greetings to Christians.[1]

When I arrive at the office, there are only two cars in the driveway, plus a number of office vans. The guard asks where I'm going. When I answer, he says that the meeting isn't until 2:00 p.m. I send a text message to managing editor Elba Damhuri, who confirms that this is true. "2:00, Janet. Merry Christmas," he writes in English. Why is this significant? Because *Republika* has a reputation for being a politically conservative newspaper, generally following the lead of the Council of Indonesian Ulama as well as Nahdlatul Ulama (NU) and Muhammadiyah, Indonesia's two largest Muslim organizations. Yet on this Christmas Day, three of the nine editors who attended the editorial meeting said "Selamat Natal," and several more shook my hand. I had brought along chocolate chip cookies, and one of the editors sent out an office boy for a round of Coca Colas and one Coke Light, making this a special occasion.

The headline story for December 26 was to be "A Peaceful Christmas in Jakarta," with page 2 stories focusing on how Muslim youth groups had in many cases provided security for Christmas celebrations and the atmosphere of tolerance and pluralism that prevailed. As one of the editors typed out ideas for the next day's edition, he noted, "This shows how Islam can also be seen as tolerant." After the meeting broke up, we stayed on for a while and chatted. I asked if they thought that anyone at *Republika* would have a problem saying "Merry Christmas" to me or to anyone else. They looked surprised. "No," they said, "definitely not." Elba Damhuri added that *Republika* often gets attacked by religious conservatives for being too liberal. For example, a few days earlier the paper had published an advertisement that contained the greeting "Selamat Natal"; Elba Damhuri said that in response he had received numerous text messages—all of them critical.

Although journalists at *Republika* may not be aware of the academic arguments that inform the debate over whether there is such a thing as "Islamic communication," they wrestle with these concerns every day. Founded in 1993, *Republika* has an explicit mission: to serve the Muslim community. With an estimated circulation of seventy thousand and a readership of perhaps two to four times that number, the newspaper reaches a largely middle-class audience of readers between the ages of twenty and forty.[2] Indonesia is frequently described as "the world's most populous Muslim country," but there has long been a feeling that despite being the numerical majority, Muslims have been marginalized. Although there is a venerable tradition of an "Islamic press" in Indonesia, these papers have generally had small circulations and been short-lived. *Republika*, a large, mass-marketed daily that has thrived for more than two decades, is an exception. According to *Republika* editors, in mid-2016 the paper continued to rank as the third most read in Indonesia.[3]

Founded in 1993 with the blessing of then-president Soeharto and the financial support of Ikatan Cendekiawan Muslim Indonesia (ICMI, the Association of Indonesian Muslim Intellectuals), *Republika* is now published by Mahaka Media, a business venture with many media holdings. Its history illustrates a number of important themes, including the relationship between journalism and Islam, the difficulties of maintaining independence under an authoritarian regime, and the advantages and disadvantages of commercialization. Today's *Republika* above all is commercial, which has had

Republika. Photo by author.

implications not only for the kinds of issues it covers but also for how it reports them. In a world of shrinking resources, aging readers, and scarce advertising dollars, all print media are aware of the bottom line. For *Republika*, however, this commercial focus reflects more than the need for survival; to a large extent, it is *Republika*'s market that determines the publication's content.

When you first enter the office of *Republika* at No. 37 Jl. Warung Buncit, it doesn't look very different from that of any other Indonesian newspaper. Oddly shaped, with a large spiral staircase, the building was originally intended to be an "entertainment venue," complete with a sauna on the fourth floor. There is nothing about it to suggest that it houses Indonesia's largest and most influential Islamic newspaper. At *Republika* there is no Islamic attire, no white robes or long beards. Although many of the female reporters and editors wear headscarves, there are some who do not. Like attending Friday prayers, "it is a private, individual matter," says Nasihin Masha, the paper's chief editor until March 2016. Irfan Junaidi, who replaced him, agrees.

Despite the lack of Islamic "symbols," there is no question that *Republika* is a newspaper with the explicit goal of serving the Muslim community.

Nasihin, now a "special editor," says that *Republika* has five basic principles: it is modern, moderate, Muslim, nationalist, and populist. Ikhwanul Kiram Mashuri, a graduate of both the modernist *pesantren* (boarding school) Gontor and Al-Azhar University in Cairo and the editor of *Republika* until 2010, is even more explicit about *Republika*'s mission as a Muslim community newspaper. In an in-house history, he wrote: "From the first page to the last . . . there is nothing outside of the framework of *amar ma'ruf nahi munkar* [inviting good and forbidding wrong]."

Scholars have argued that in Islam "inviting good and forbidding wrong" is paramount and that Muslims have an obligation to stop evil when they see it (Cook 2003). But how are such abstract principles implemented in practical journalism? Journalists at *Republika* speak of the need to be *inspiratif* (inspiring). As managing editor Elba Damhuri explains, in practice this means not only reporting on conditions as they are but also giving inspiration as to how they should be. This is what makes *Republika* different from other media. "This is what I mean by 'substantial' Islam," he said. "We cannot stand by and watch our neighbors, who are poor, this is wrong. We cannot see churches burned. This is not permitted. We cannot allow Ahmadiyah communities to be burned.[4] We work because we have something to say: tolerance. This is substantial Islam."

When Syahruddin El Fikri, a senior editor at *Republika*, compares his paper with other Indonesian newspapers like *Tempo*—a majority of whose journalists are also Muslim—he agrees that the religious creed of the journalists is the same. But what will be different, he suggests, is *Republika*'s focus on solutions. When there is violence against Ahmadiyah, *Tempo* will cover it by focusing on the lack of tolerance. "We see it from a different perspective," Syahruddin said. "We look to create a solution, not add to the anxiety [*kegelisahan*]. *Tempo* will likewise focus on the problem of corruption. Yes, we have to shine a light on corruption, but how do we find a solution? How can it be solved in a positive way? In this manner, we are very different."

THE ASSOCIATION OF INDONESIAN MUSLIM INTELLECTUALS, *REPUBLIKA*, AND THE PRESS IN THE NEW ORDER

The history of *Republika* is profoundly connected with the history of the press in modern Indonesia, and with the end of authoritarianism. It also intersects with the history of *Tempo* in some interesting ways. When in 1993 the Association of Indonesian Muslim Intellectuals (Ikatan Cendekiawan

Muslim Indonesia, ICMI) sought permission to publish a newspaper, it was fortunate to be able to draw upon the staff of *Berita Buana*, a paper that had been shut down one year earlier by an owner who feared that his permit to run a press publication company (Surat Izin Usaha Penerbitan Pers, SIUPP) would be withdrawn. *Berita Buana* was founded in 1945 and had gone through a number of incarnations, one of which included being revitalized by a group of journalists who had left *Tempo* in the early 1990s. Their idea had been to create a newspaper that was aimed at the Muslim community but "didn't carry the flag of Islam."[5] Zaim Uchrowi, who was one of the leaders of this group explained: "We thought there was an untapped market—urban Muslims. In the previous era there had been the newspaper *Abadi*, and before that in the 1970s there was *Duta Masyarakat*. But both of them were gone. So we thought, we can make a newspaper like *Kompas*. Although the dominant community was Islam, we didn't want it to be an 'Islamic newspaper.' It was to be a regular newspaper. Because we didn't have a SIUPP at the time, we tried to find a newspaper with which we could cooperate. And that paper was *Berita Buana*."

One of the ex-*Tempo* journalists who joined the new *Berita Buana* was Farid Gaban, a gifted writer who, along with Zaim, has been credited with bringing *Tempo*'s style of journalism to the newspaper. With ex-*Tempo* journalists like Farid Gaban, Zaim Uchrowi, Abdul Rachman, and Budiono Dharsono, ICMI was thus able to draw upon a highly professional stable of journalists who had been trained in the style of *Tempo* and were known for their integrity and hard-hitting reporting.

ICMI also had a complex history. Founded in 1990 and under the chairmanship of the minister of research and technology, B. J. Habibie, ICMI was an unlikely mix of independent intellectuals, activists, and government bureaucrats who hoped to curry favor with the regime. Many of its critics considered it to be little more than a vehicle for Habibie's political aspirations or indeed for Soeharto's own reelection in 1993 (Hefner 1993, 25). Founded at a time when Soeharto was making a series of overtures to the Muslim community—especially the rapidly growing urban middle class—many viewed ICMI with skepticism, seeing it as a tool of the regime, "an instrument designed and used by President Suharto for his own purposes" (Liddle 1996a, 615). With the benefit of hindsight, historian Rémy Madinier (2015) has suggested that the reality was more complex and that within ICMI there were three groups struggling for "moral leadership" of the organization.

These were regime technocrats, who were aligned either with Habibie or the political organization Golkar; modernist intellectuals, such as Nurcholish Madjid, who hoped for the expansion of Islamic social values; and Muslim leaders, such as Amien Rais and Adi Sasono, who had political ambitions of their own (ibid., 441).

From the beginning, ICMI had hoped to establish a newspaper that would represent the entire Muslim community, and when the SIUPP belonging to *Berita Buana* became available, the organization wasted no time in obtaining it, along with the newspaper. Although ICMI did contain some exclusivist and sectarian elements, when its more progressive wing combined with the former *Berita Buana* journalists, they were able to create a newspaper that was known in its early days for a kind of "cosmopolitan Islam" that indirectly challenged the authoritarianism of the regime that had sponsored it.[6] Despite the obvious political pressures, *Republika* journalists were committed to creating a newspaper that was "tolerant, plural, and modern, as well as pious and critical" (Hefner 1997b, 97).

During its first few years, *Republika* was the vessel for a remarkable range of Islamic discourse, especially in the pages of the weekly Dialog Jumat (Friday dialogue). With an editorial board and council made up of some of Indonesia's most respected Muslim scholars, including Nurcholish Madjid, Haider Bagir, and Amien Rais, the editors and writers were a who's who of Muslim intellectuals. ICMI also recruited writers from Majelis Singergi Kalam, ICMI's think tank, for the newspaper's research and development team. One member of this group was Ade Armando, now a lecturer in the Department of Communication at the University of Indonesia, who confirmed that the term *Islam kosmopolitan* was frequently used at the time. "Cosmopolitan Islam was a brand," he said, "a brand that we used to differentiate ourselves from other groups. It was Islam that valued openness, Islam that was ready for democracy, and Islam that valued human rights."

Former *Republika* journalist Daru Priyambodo, who now works for *Tempo* newspaper, recalled that the paper's R&D team were "young ICMI with moderate thinking, who believed that this nation had to be educated to understand tolerant Islam." He added: "People said that this was a dream team for *Republika*, because they were young thinkers who were generally more like Nurcholish Madjid. They were with his *aliran* or stream." Daru continued: "The term [cosmopolitan Islam] was often used in conversations between us. The kind of Islam we tried to serve with [*Republika*] was cosmopolitan and urban. We wanted an Islam that was educated, open-minded, and that understood Islamic values. And that wasn't too quick to say that the other person is *kafir* [unbeliever/infidel]! But we weren't able to succeed, because there was too much pressure from other Islamic groups."

The problem with being ICMI's newspaper was that everyone thought they owned a piece of it, including such conservative groups as Dewan Dakwah Islamiyah Indonesia (DDII), the Indonesian Council for Islamic Propagation, which was unhappy with the kinds of articles and opinion pieces that the newspaper published. DDII represented a politically conservative strain of reformist Islam that had its intellectual forebears in the banned political party Masyumi (Majelis Syuro Muslimin Indonesia, or the Indonesian Muslim Consultative Council), and most specifically in the thinking of Mohammad Natsir (Hefner 1997b, 80–81). "For one or two years, *Republika* was published with a vision that was more open, moderate, and sometimes even seen as secular," Daru said, "but the hardliner groups felt that *Republika* should be their newspaper. When they saw the stories that were made by *Republika*, they said, 'That's not what we want. This is not what we wanted!' And there were editorials that made this group angry."

One such editorial, written by Hamid Basyaib, who was later one of the founders of the Liberal Islamic Network, commented on the 1995 death of a beautiful young Indonesian starlet and singer named Nike Ardilla. When Hamid concluded with the hope that Nike was now sleeping at the side of God, Daru continued, the reaction was immediate: "For us, the first generation of *Republika*, there was no problem with this sentence. But for others, they were angry! How can you write a sentence that says that God is sleeping with a woman? They were angry! This was not the kind of newspaper we wanted, they said! So we were *demo-demo*."

The struggle within the military between the "green" (Islamic) and "red" (nationalist) groups who were both vying for Soeharto's attention during the last years of the New Order has been well documented (Hefner 2000, 151), and this was reflected in *Republika* as well. Burhan Sholihin, a *Tempo* newspaper journalist who began his career at *Republika*, said, "*Republika* had difficulty because it had to become an umbrella for all Islamic groups, from those who were moderate to those who were hardliners. During the first few years, this problem didn't really emerge, because everybody was accommodated. But as the political situation became more chaotic, the pressure became more intense."

On May 29, 1997, the exact date of the Indonesian election, Muhammadiyah head Amien Rais wrote a column titled "Kejujuran" (Honesty), in which he called upon "all of us, the people, the government, and those running the election," to uphold honesty and justice (quoted in Utomo 2010, 31). According to Daru Priyambodo: "Soeharto was very angry, and he demanded that the chief editor be changed. And Parni Hadi [the chief editor] stepped down, and was exchanged with a Habibie man who had no background in journalism. He was a good person, but he was asked to keep an eye on things so that nothing was published that would make Habibie angry, Soeharto angry, or the military angry. When this happened, for those of us inside, it was hopeless."

COMMERCIAL MEDIA AND THE INDONESIAN MIDDLE CLASS

In 2010, *Republika* celebrated its seventeenth birthday with the publication of an in-house history (Utomo 2010). In that book the newspaper's history is divided into two periods: the "political" period under ICMI and the "business" period under Mahaka. In 1999, after B. J. Habibie was defeated in the presidential election, *Republika* foundered. Despite its progressive elements, ICMI had been a creature of the Soeharto regime. Times had changed, and *Republika* needed a new investor. In 2000, Mahaka Media bought *Republika* and changed its economic basis, if not its Islamic orientation. Pointing out that one reason for the frequent failures of Islamic media in Indonesia was that they hadn't been built on a sound financial footing, Mahaka CEO Erick Thohir promised that *Republika* would continue to serve the Muslim community but on a commercial basis. With a new emphasis on advertising and marketing, the paper would thrive.

To a very large extent, this has happened. The newspaper is now a successful business venture. As the in-house history notes, *Republika* has dispelled the myth that Islamic media is a poor place in which to advertise. Today's readers are from Indonesia's urban middle class, comfortable with both their religious values and a more consumption-oriented lifestyle (Robison 1996; Dick 1990). In this way *Republika* also reflects what Indonesia specialist Ariel Heryanto (2011, 60–82) has described as the new Muslim middle-class values apparent in the beautiful clothes and exotic locations of the pious tearjerker and hit film *Ayat Ayat Cinta* (Verses of love). Perhaps not coincidentally, *Ayat Ayat Cinta* was first published in *Republika* as a serial story and later as a novel (El Shirazy 2004).

Of course not everyone was happy with these changes, and those who felt the most marginalized were the ones who had upheld the values of cosmopolitan Islam. As Ade Armando put it, the people "who not only wanted to give inspiration to Muslim groups but also wanted our Islam to color Indonesia in the right manner, [who were looking] for a market that was democratic, who cared about social issues, who didn't see Islam as something tied to the past, and who wanted an Islam that was pluralist, now that group was slowly marginalized, and then left."

At a noisy New Year's Eve gathering in Menteng, former *Tempo* chief editor Bambang Harymurti, learning about my research at *Republika*, commented that he had at one time been a regular reader of *Republika* back when it had been a voice for cosmopolitan Islam. When did that change? I asked. "When they all moved to *Koran Tempo*!" he said. Later, I asked Burhan and Daru if what Bambang had said was true. Burhan laughed. "The groups that struggled for cosmopolitan Islam *pindah semua* [all moved]!" he said. According to Ade Armando, who stopped writing for *Republika* in 2005: "I think that [*Republika*'s] cosmopolitan Islam is now more connected with cooking, life styles, and building a modern economy."

ISLAM AS A MARKET NICHE

Everyone knows that *Republika* is read mostly by men.[7] Surveys suggest this, as do the letters to the editor and the newspaper's own informal research. For several years, starting in 2012, *Republika* published a special Tuesday supplement called "Leisure" that was aimed at women. Although the supplement has recently been folded into the Sunday edition as well as daily pages on shopping, travel, and health, the section is nevertheless worth examining for what it suggests about the newspaper's perspective on women, Islam, and consumption. The Leisure section contained interesting and readable articles on fashion, food, travel, and beauty tips. Although the supplement had a section called "Hijabbers' Corner," not all of the models in Leisure were shown wearing hijab (head scarves). Section editor Indira Rezkisari, who joined *Republika* in 2005, said that although there were occasional complaints about this, those with truly "narrow views" probably didn't read the newspaper in the first place. What was important was appropriateness. "Generally, we can't have sleeveless," she said. "On our cover we cannot have cleavage or thighs, but calves are okay. All fashion doesn't have to be Muslim."

The same goes for food, she continued:

> At the meeting the other day, there was the issue of halal/non-halal food. I'll give you an example. We wanted to have a story about Japanese food. A lot of it contains sake. So during the interview we asked can you have food without sake? And we wrote in the story that you can by special request. If you want to eat without sake, the chef can make it by request.
>
> Similarly, if the restaurant has both halal and non-halal foods, we ask if the wok is the same, the chopping board, are they separate? I know that there are several hotels in Indonesia that use international protocols and keep them separate, so that our readers who care will know. There are some of them of course who don't care.

The newspaper's stance on individual choice is deliberate. Sara, a young reporter for the Leisure section, said, "When I am in the field, nearly each time I say that I am from *Republika*, the first question is, '*Kok ngak pakai hijab?*' [Why no head scarf?] Nearly every time. Nearly every time!" When I asked Sara how she answered, she said, "It depends on who asked. But usually I say, '*Tidak diwajibkan.*' [It's not required]. Although we are indeed an Islamic newspaper, in matters of appearance we are not that rigid. We are flexible." Senior editor Subroto confirmed this position. "When we recruit, we don't consider religion," he said. "You can wear a *jilbab* or not, it's up to you. Praying too—if you want to pray or not, it's up to you. It's a private matter. Here there are those who are very [pious], and there are also those who are secular fundamentalists. There are all types."

Each Monday afternoon there is a weekly meeting that includes editors from all the special pages and supplements, including Gen-I (aimed mainly at twenty-somethings), Islam Digest (Islamic history, along with different aspects of Islamic civilization), and Dialog Jumat. The atmosphere at this meeting, which is made up almost entirely of women, is markedly different from the daily editorial meeting, which is dominated by men. When I observed the meeting on January 21, 2013, it was presided over by assistant managing editor Subroto, who noted jovially that yes, he had learned to "accommodate himself" to the female atmosphere. After joking that "at this meeting we cover everything from fashion to the hereafter," he explained that

Halal bihalal at *Republika*, 2014. Photo by author.

the Leisure pages are something that can be enjoyed by all. "We wanted something that can serve all our readers," he said. "We were too masculine. Our readers are educated; Islam doesn't have to be stiff—it can be modern. The image of Islam doesn't have to be harsh. We want to build a house for all groups."

What differentiates the Leisure pages from women's sections in other newspapers is the context of *Republika* itself. As editor Indira Rezkisari noted, "I'm sure our readers read the other sections, including Islam Digest and Dialog Jumat." Of course, she said, "our readers don't pray all the time! Whatever we do, we have to do it as well as possible. This is our guide. Our readers may need the Hadith, but you don't need a Hadith or a sermon to teach you how to shop. Life is more than just praying. You also wear clothes, travel, etc."

Although it is seldom acknowledged explicitly, for the newspaper routinely to include photographs of women without headscarves on the cover of its Leisure pages is a political statement. What is acknowledged explicitly is the ability of these supplements to attract new advertisers as well as new readers. As editor Indira Rezkisari put it: "When Leisure was a concept, we thought of women from the middle class and above. We thought this would be a good way of appealing to advertisers, and so far they have come from banks, something that before you wouldn't have seen much of in *Republika*. Because we focus on shopping, credit cards have entered. Because we have stories on travel, banks put in ads saying you can take out money wherever you are!"

The question of *Republika*'s relationship with advertisers and its editorial autonomy has come up more than once, most directly in a book published by the Indonesian office of the German political foundation Friedrich Ebert Stiftung (Keller 2009). Comparing four Indonesian newspapers—*Kompas*, *Tempo*, *Media Indonesia*, and *Republika*—researcher Anett Keller concluded that at both *Republika* and *Media Indonesia*—papers in which the owners had "no journalistic experience"—there was considerable meddling in editorial matters, especially those pertaining to the owners' business partners. Of the four, only *Tempo* was found to have clear guidelines separating business from editorial interests as well as a willingness even "to risk that advertising clients might be surprised by critical stories." The other papers were found to have no such policies (ibid., 104–7). Although Keller's findings caused considerable consternation at *Republika*, they were difficult to deny, especially given that one of her sources had been owner Erick Thohir himself.

"PAK ERICK"

Erick Thohir is a charming businessman. Outgoing and amiable, he met me in February 2013 for an early Friday night dinner at the Goods Diner, a trendy place in South Jakarta. "Are you a Muslim?" he asked shortly after we found a place at a table. It was the first time that anyone had ever asked me that. After I responded "no," Erick Thohir said, "The first time I entered *Republika* I gave them a photo. This is Islam! [The person] was German, but Islam! Therefore don't think, a Chinese person, a white person is not a Muslim. It is not certain. You cannot be prejudiced." When I asked about his own religious beliefs, he said, "I am a Haji! But certainly, Islam for my family is something personal. It is our identity, but it is something personal. My father is from Lampung—half Lampung, half Bugis from Makassar. My mother is half Chinese, half West Java, and Muslim. Very Indonesian. My brother married with Padang, my sister married with Jawa Timor. I married with half Chinese, half Betawi."

Erick Thohir makes no secret of his business interests. "I always ask them [journalists at *Republika*], 'What's the biggest market?' " He continues:

I remember four messages I gave when I entered *Republika*. The first, *Republika* should be in the center, moderate. Number 2, I don't want Islam to be considered stupid, to not have money, to be backward. I don't want this. The third, we cannot be prejudiced. When we see something, we can't automatically be negative. We have to have an open mind. And the last one, the one I want, is what I said before. You have to think about the readers, the viewers, the market, the big market.

What were my four points? One, business of course. The second, stay in the middle. The third, business to business, think of the market. And the fourth, don't be prejudiced. Anti-globalization? It hasn't been proved to be bad! Don't think of it as bad. Something foreign? Not proven bad. Don't think of it as bad. Foreigners pay taxes. Therefore I say be positive.

Despite what is undoubtedly Erick Thohir's positive outlook, he remains controversial. As former *Republika* writer Ade Armando said matter-of-factly, "When Erick Thohir entered, he truly intended to use it as an opportunity to develop his new business. At the time he was a young man, and he was filthy rich (*kaya raya*), and he wanted to spend money on things that would be profitable. For him, it was a business opportunity."

As the president director of Beyond Media, a holding company for Mahaka Media, the forty-six-year-old businessman is the owner of three lifestyle and sports magazines, two newspapers (*Harian Sin Chew Indonesia* and *Republika*), four radio stations, and a television station (Jak-TV).[8] Erick Thohir is also the president director of TVOne, which he owns with Golkar chief Aburizal Bakrie. A huge sports fan, Thohir is part owner of the Philadelphia 76ers and the professional soccer team DC United. Although nearly everyone at *Republika* will admit that the newspaper pays special attention to Pak Erick's basketball team, they also insist that this is the only arena in which he has any influence.

Deputy managing editor Joko Sadewo said, "Up until now, the ownership doesn't intervene with us concerning sensitive issues. We have agreed upon that. The issue of corruption, whoever does it, we will write about it. This is our agreement." Joko Sadewo added with a laugh: "Actually, he is a basketball owner—but this is not a sensitive topic. He owns shares in the Philadelphia 76ers. Pak Erick is very interested in sports." Former chief editor Ikhwanul Kiram Mashuri said much the same thing: "Yes, it's true, that it's only sports. If it's something about politics, what happens is that there is a discussion, with me and whoever from editorial. And there is a mutual discussion, and then the attitude is taken, as a result of the discussion, but it is not always his [Erick's] opinion that we take."

When asked about Thohir's part ownership of TVOne, *Republika*'s editors insist that Pak Erick's partnership with Golkar party chief Aburizal Bakrie has nothing at all to do with their newspaper. As is well known, TVOne played a major role in the 2014 presidential election, openly supporting Gen. Prabowo Subianto over Joko Widodo and then on election night refusing to concede defeat (Tapsell 2015, 47–48). The presidential election created controversy for *Republika*, although in all likelihood it had less to do with Erick Thohir than it did with the news organization's market. *Republika* was widely perceived to support Prabowo.[9] Even longtime *Republika* columnist and former UIN Jakarta rector Azyumardi Azra said that he and his children believed the paper was supporting Prabowo and Islamist PKS (Partai Keadilan Sejahtera, the Prosperous Justice Party). Then-chief editor Nasihin Masha denied this, saying that before the campaign began, he had gathered the reporters and editors and told them, "Our policy is that *Republika* supports both. We are not neutral, we support both of them." Yet even casual perusal of *Republika Online* (ROL) headlines showed overwhelming support for the Golkar candidate. Why?

There are several possible explanations, all of them having to do with *Republika*'s market. Joko Sadewo, who was the editor of ROL during the campaign, bridled at the suggestion that *Republika* was biased toward Prabowo. Pointing out that "it is a rule of *Republika* that we can't side with one candidate," he said the perception that *Republika* favored Prabowo sometimes made it difficult to get quotes from Jokowi's camp. More important, Joko Sadewo noted that because most of the ROL readers are from Muhammadiyah, they liked stories that attacked Jokowi. Once readers clicked on those stories, they went to the top of the "most popular" list and then got even more hits. "This was automatic," Joko Sadewo said. "ROL wasn't controlling it." The process was amplified even more when people saw these stories on

Facebook and Twitter. "This was a part of [the Prabowo camp's] cyber-war, their cyber armies," he said. "Their cyber-armies worked to push out these stories, so it looked as if *Republika* was pro-Prabowo."

Joko Sadewo is right about this. His observations about the relationship between web analytics and the traditional gatekeeping process has been noted by many media scholars (Tandoc 2014). As he pointed out, the results of ROL's informal "daily survey" showed that readers of the website favored Prabowo by a factor of about 6 to 1. "These are the readers," he said, "and these are the people who pushed the stories in favor of Prabowo and against Jokowi to the top." When I asked Joko Sadewo and several other editors which candidate most of the journalists at *Republika* had supported, the answer was about 50 percent for Jokowi, about 50 percent for Prabowo. Although this might surprise some of *Republika*'s critics, it brings us back to the central paradox: everything at *Republika* is market-driven.

Is *Republika* a better, more independent newspaper now that it is run on a commercial basis than it was under the controlled press of the Soeharto years? This question is difficult to answer. On the surface, it is obvious that as with the rest of the Indonesian press, the news that is published in *Republika* is much more comprehensive and hard-hitting now than before. The kinds of issues that the paper reports on—corruption, poverty, politics, and economics—are done with an openness and vigor that was simply not possible during the Soeharto years (Romano 2003). Yet at the same time, it is clear that *Republika*'s market segment has become more important and drives story selection. As former chief editor Nasihin Masha explained, "Like toothpaste," each media has its own segment, and *Republika* is a Muslim community newspaper. As a result, the paper focuses more on Islamic political parties and matters of interest to the Muslim community than one would find in other Indonesian newspapers. Anything deemed "pornographic," including photos of women in skimpy clothing, is completely off-limits.[10] One frequently hears the statement that *Republika* is a family newspaper, something that everyone in the house should be comfortable reading.

It is instructive to compare the post-ICMI *Republika* with *Tempo* newspaper (*Koran Tempo*), which was established in 2001 and employs a number of ex-*Republika* journalists who left the paper during the upheaval that occurred around the time of the ownership change. Both papers have attractive, modern designs and use clear, straightforward language. The most readily apparent difference is *Republika*'s position on issues touching on freedom of expression.

Whereas a number of *Republika* journalists may not personally object to Indonesian *Playboy* magazine, Lady Gaga, or discussions of the biography of Canadian-lesbian-Muslim writer Irshad Manji, the newspaper as an institution opposes them. The reverse is true at *Tempo*. Why? For *Republika*'s journalists the explanation is clear: "because of our readers."

In Dialog Jumat and the other supplements that focus on religion, *Republika* appears unwilling to take on controversial positions that run the risk of offending the readers. Whereas in the early 1990s, the Friday Dialogue section incorporated a wide range of opinion, including those of feminists, religious "liberals," experts on human rights, and even non-Muslims, today's sections on religion cater to the majority view. For example, during a 2013 controversy over a fatwa by the Indonesian Council of Ulama (Majelis Ulama Indonesia, MUI) against the banning of female circumcision, *Republika* stayed out of the debate. Although the controversy was widely reported in other Indonesian media, *Republika* published only a page 12 news story on the fatwa. Editors said they were unlikely to follow up with additional coverage on their "Pro/Kontra" page.[11] In a small discussion with editors, the consensus was that reporting on the "pros and cons" of female circumcision was "too much bother" and that the issue had already been covered. "We can debate about this endlessly, or we can just agree to stop debating," said one editor. "It's counterproductive," said another. "It's just wasting time."[12]

More recently, *Republika* has taken a harsh stance on rights for the LGBT community. Sparked by a January 2016 statement from the Ministry of Education opposing a decision by the University of Indonesia to allow a support group for gay and lesbian students, members of Parliament from the Prosperous Justice Party (Partai Keadilan Sejahtera, PKS) said they would propose an anti-LGBT bill that would ban gay rights activism and criminalize LGBT behavior. On January 24, *Republika* jumped into the fray with a page 1 story under the headline "LGBT Ancaman Serius" (LGBT a serious threat). As *Republika*'s editor Irfan Junaida was quick to point out, although the story did not advocate killing, hatred, or any other kind of violence, it nevertheless reinforced the idea—expressed by the religious and educational authorities it quoted—that advocates of homosexuality on campus and in the mass media were causing the LGBT lifestyle to spread "faster than narcotics" and even as far as elementary and middle schools.[13]

The story provoked an immediate outcry from human rights activists, and a January 29 *somasi* (summons) to the Press Council from the Lesbian,

Gay, Bisexual, Transgender, Intersex, and Questioning Forum (LGBTIQ), which claimed that the story violated the press code of ethics by spreading hatred.[14] Far from backing down, *Republika* ran additional stories. On February 18, Dompet Dhuafa (Fund for the Underprivileged), *Republika's* nonprofit social and humanitarian wing, sponsored a forum that included psychologists and legal experts, a representative from the Indonesian child protection commission, religious leaders from MUI, Dewan Dakwah, Nahdlatul Ulama, and Muhammadiyah, along with several "reformed" gays. Their conclusion was unanimous: homosexuality was an aberration if not a choice or a psychological disorder, and the only way to fix it was to return to one's "true nature" (*fitra*) as a man or woman. The program was called "Embrace the Victims of LGBT, Reject the Legalization of LGBT."[15]

Like the lack of debate on the topic of female circumcision, *Republika's* stance on LGBT rights reveals much about the newspaper's orientation and the perceived orientation of its readers. Nearly four years of fieldwork and monitoring of *Republika* suggest that many of the journalists who work at the news organization do not share the views that their paper projects. As many of them have told me privately, "it's the readers." Just as the readers drove the paper's perceived support of Prabowo and criticism of Jokowi, they have pushed the news organization into positions that are increasingly politically conservative. Indeed, it is possible that when the paper was subsidized by ICMI, it may have been freer to lead the Muslim community by providing a wide range of viewpoints. Although today's *Republika* journalists point proudly to how Erick Thohir and Mahaka have taken *Republika* out of politics and placed it on a sound business footing, it is hard not to conclude that the newspaper has paid a price for this shift toward commercialization, now repeating the conventional wisdom rather than challenging the perceived interests of either the readers or the advertisers.

JOURNALISM, ISLAM, DEMOCRACY

In the words of managing editor Elba Damhuri, it is a "dilemma" to run an Islamic newspaper in Indonesia, because nobody agrees on what Islam should be. Even a simple question such as when the fasting month of Ramadan ends can be problematic, as Indonesia's two largest religious organizations, Muhammadiyah and Nahdlatul Ulama, frequently celebrate Eid at different times.[16] As newsroom editor Asep K Nurzaman explained, one definition of tolerance is "how to live peacefully, not only between religions but also between NU and Muhammadiyah." Assistant managing editor Heri Ruslan, who was once the editor of *Republika Online* (ROL), likewise said that there are many different *mazhab* (schools) in Indonesian Islam and that each one thinks it is right. "So no matter what ROL includes, someone is angry," he said. "They complain via Twitter and Facebook, and urge others to stop subscribing."

Since its founding, *Republika* has had to handle pressure from both inside Islam and outside it. With a mixture of pride and ruefulness, *Republika* journalists can recite a list of the occasions on which the newspaper has been demonstrated against, even by Islamic organizations that have objected to something published. The tolerance and pluralism that *Republika* officially celebrates, which could be seen in its editors' willingness to extend Christmas greetings to a non-Muslim, are marks of the kind of communal tolerance that political scientist Jeremy Menchik (2016) observed in his study of Indonesian Islamic organizations. As the 2010 Arab Spring witnessed numerous majority Muslim nations struggling to throw off the chains of authoritarianism, many commentators noted that Indonesia has much to teach the world about Islam and democracy (Pintak and Setiyono 2011). Although the advantages and disadvantages of *Republika*'s commercial model can be debated, its success suggests that as a large, modern newspaper serving the Muslim community, *Republika* has much to offer. Despite the trade-offs in the transition from political to commercial, *Republika* continues to serve up a style of professional journalism that speaks for democracy and economic justice. The question, however, remains: Is *Republika* serving the interests of its Muslim readers, or pandering to them?

THREE

HARAKAH

Political Islam

IT IS Christmas Eve 2014, and I'm having coffee with Zulkifli Sulong, the jolly, bespectacled former editor of *Harakah* newspaper and *HarakahDaily.net* at a shopping mall in Kuala Lumpur. His party, the Pan-Malaysian Islamic Party (Parti Islam Se-Malaysia, PAS), is about to split over what seems to be the issue of who will be the new chief minister of the state of Selangor. This is misleading, however, as the dispute is really about whether the party should be led by the ulama faction of religious scholars or by the "professionals."

Harakah, which is owned by PAS, has not reported on any of this. "So of course, we don't like that!" Zulkifli says. "Because every other media reports on the issue, but we don't know the PAS version! What is the real truth? So this makes a problem for the readers. They can get the info from the other papers, but this is our news area, what we should report. Instead, they have to hear it from somebody else." I ask, "If you were still the editor, would you have been able to report on what was really happening in the party?" Zulkifli says, "I would fight! If the directive came from the chairman of *Harakah*, or maybe the board of directors, I would go straight to them, 'How come our members can't get the real truth from PAS?' So as a journalist, I would have fought. Of course they would have kept a very close eye on us, but I think if we just discussed the news, they would not—the problem comes if you spin. But if you give the real news, nobody will be against you."

It can be difficult enough for any Muslim reporter to reconcile the teachings of Islam with the principles of good journalism, but journalists who also have to keep the interests of a political party in mind—especially when that party itself is divided—face an almost impossible task. This was the dilemma

Former *Harakah* editor Zulkifli Sulong, 2017. Photo courtesy of Saidah Ali.

faced by the editors of *Harakah*, the newspaper of the Pan-Malaysian Islamic Party, which political scientist Farish Noor (2014, 10) described as "one of the most prominent—if not *the* most prominent—Islamist party in Malaysia and Southeast Asia today." For almost thirty years *Harakah*, which means "the movement," managed somehow to balance these different considerations, but by the end of 2015 the news organization's future looked doubtful, as a crisis within the party led to the resignation and sidelining of *Harakah*'s most experienced editors and professional journalists. The story of how the paper managed to survive for as long as it did, and to garner the respect it had as an alternative newspaper, shatters many assumptions about what "Islamic media" looks like. Although it initially seemed possible to reconcile Islamic teachings with good journalism, the interests of the political party ultimately proved to be much harder to incorporate, especially when one faction of PAS came to be at loggerheads with its coalition partner, the Democratic Action Party (DAP), over the issue of Hudud (the penalties for a specific set of criminal offenses under the Islamic legal code). The most controversial of these penalties include the cutting off of the hand for theft and stoning for adultery.

To understand the significance of *Harakah* and the role it has played, it is necessary to understand not only the political party that owns the paper but also the struggle over political Islam in modern Malaysia. The twists and turns that have occurred in the relationship between the Islamic party and its biggest rival (and sometime partner), the United Malays National Organization (UMNO), are a significant part of the complex and frequently dispiriting struggle for a democratic Malaysia. Since it was first established in 1987, *Harakah*'s editors have struggled to serve the party while at the same time practicing good journalism and being true to the teachings of Islam. It was never easy, and by mid-2015, when the resurgent "ulama faction" purged the party of the "professionals"—who in turn threatened to establish a new party—it appeared that the news organization was an experiment that had failed. Or, as Zulkifli Sulong explained: "When the people start to move away from PAS, they will stop buying *Harakah*."

THE PAN-MALAYSIAN ISLAMIC PARTY

PAS was founded in 1951. Originally the religious wing of the United Malays National Organization, it split with the larger party over the issues of race and religion that continue to vex Malaysia today. In the eyes of the ulama (religious scholars) who established PAS, UMNO, devoted as it was to uniting the Malays and working toward independence, did not do enough to prioritize Islam and the idea of an Islamic state. Although PAS would eventually accuse UMNO of an un-Islamic ethnocentric nationalism and advocate Islam as the solution to a plural society (Jomo and Cheek 1992, 98), the Islamic party has not been consistent in this stand.

A key question that comes up with any study of Islamist political movements is how compatible is the goal of the Islamic state with democratic institutions? Would it be possible to build an Islamic state that not only promotes genuine tolerance of non-Muslims but also guarantees them an equal role in political and civil life? How do Muslims reconcile a commitment to sharia—including Hudud—with the culture of the modern world? In this way, disagreements about the role of *Harakah* (which coincide with the conflict between the ulama and professional factions of PAS) mirror what political scientist Carrie Wickham (2013, 58–70) has found to be the conflict between the more conservative old guard and the middle-generation reformers of the Egyptian Muslim Brotherhood.

These parallels are not incidental. Scholars of Southeast Asia have long focused on the ties between Islam in Southeast Asia and the Middle East (Azra 1999; Tagliacozzo 2009). Steamship travel and the opening of the Suez Canal in the late nineteenth century made the Hajj far more affordable for Muslim pilgrims and allowed for increased intellectual contact between Muslims of the Malay Archipelago and scholars in the two most important centers of Islamic thought: Mecca and Cairo. Al-Azhar's Sheik Muhammad 'Abduh and his disciple Rashid Rida influenced a generation of young Muslims who studied in Cairo at the turn of the twentieth century (H. Zakaria 2007), while the Arab-language publication *Al-Manar* (The lighthouse) likewise inspired the establishment of a number of short-lived newspapers in the Straits Settlements that were edited by Malayan Muslims (Azra 1999; Roff 1967).

Al-Manar was primarily focused on the weaknesses of Muslim political institutions, the damage wrought by European colonialism, and the notion that Islam was compatible with modernity (Abushouk 2007, 303). These issues would also preoccupy Muslim journalists in the Straits Settlements, and *Harakah*—with its rejection of what PAS regarded as the ruling coalition's morally bankrupt development policies, widespread corruption, and hardening of class interests (Peletz 2002, 246)—can be seen as the descendent of these publications.

More recently, the Muslim Brotherhood, which traces its intellectual roots to the same reform sentiment in Islam that was propagated by 'Abduh and Rida, has drawn considerable scholarly attention but mostly in studies of the Arab world (Nada and Thompson 2012; Rubin 2010; Wickham 2013). Although scholars who write about the late-twentieth-century wave of piety and growth of political Islam in Southeast Asia acknowledge the influence of the ideas of the Brotherhood, it is generally only in passing (Liow 2009, 8; Bubalo and Fealy 2005, 64–74; Jomo and Cheek 1992, 85). A recent exception is researcher Zulkifly Malek (2011), who suggests that much like the earlier waves of Islamic thought, the transmission of Brotherhood ideology to the Malay Archipelago occurred largely as the result of personal connections. Although several future PAS leaders made direct contact with Hasan Al-Banna and Sayid Qutb in the 1940s and 1950s, it was activists in the Muslim Youth Movement of Malaysia (Angkatan Belia Islam Malaysia, ABIM) that embraced the Muslim Brotherhood's bottom-up view of Islamization, focusing on Islamic revivalism through renewal and reform rather than the top-down establishment of an Islamic state (Malek 2011, 17–21). Many of these ABIM activists, including Abdul Hadi Awang and Fadhil Noor, later became leaders in PAS (Jomo and Cheek 1988).

Contact between PAS and the Muslim Brotherhood continued on into the 1960s, as several Brotherhood members fled to Malaya after the organization's banning by the Egyptian government. In 1963, PAS sent future president Yusuf Rawa to Egypt and Iraq to "introduce PAS as an Islamist movement and establish relations with the Islamist movements there." This mission resulted in ten scholarships for young Malays to further their studies in Baghdad. While these students—which included both a future PAS youth chief and deputy president—were in Iraq studying Islamic law and Arabic philosophy, they were also "formally trained in the ways of the Muslim Brotherhood" (Malek 2011, 22–24).

The ideas of the Muslim Brotherhood were also disseminated through translations—future PAS president Yusuf Rawa himself translated Sayid Qutb's *In the Shade of the Quran*—and such short-lived periodicals as a magazine called *Al-Nur* (The light), which was published by students at the University of Malaya under the tutelage of an Arabic language instructor who was also a Muslim Brotherhood member (Malek 2011, 29–30). More recently, the official spokesman of the Muslim Brotherhood urged Malaysians to support PAS in the 2008 general election (ibid., 74). After the surprising upset by the opposition parties, UMNO leaders approached PAS covertly and proposed "unity governments" consisting of the two majority Malay parties for the states of Perak and Selangor, in which DAP had won the most seats, leaving PAS a minority partner in any opposition coalition. Malek (ibid., 75) wrote: "[PAS president] Abdul Hadi Awang left for London to seek advice from the Muslim Brotherhood leaders on the right course of action for PAS. The advice he received was never divulged, but the unity government never materialized."

POLITICIZATION OF ISLAM

As the secret negotiations between PAS president Hadi Awang and UMNO suggest, Malaysian Islam is indeed what anthropologist Judith Nagota (2010, 27) has called "unavoidably political." Although the rights of different categories of citizens are enshrined in Article 3 of the Constitution, Malaysia's official religion is Islam, and the state has the last word on matters of religion. Because Malays are Muslim by definition and thus required to adhere to the sharia, in practice freedom of religion for Malays is limited to choices within Islam. Much of this can be traced to the legacy of British colonialism, which strengthened and even institutionalized the relationship between Islam and the state. As historian William Roff (1967, 67) has explained: "Prior to the protectorate period, Islam in Malaya had not, in any effective sense, been a 'state religion.' There was a general awareness that all Malays were Muslims and that this distinguished them from, for example, Chinese or Siamese. To undergo conversion to Islam was in fact to masok Melayu, 'become a Malay,' but this identification of ethnic group with religion was of future rather than present significance. In the realm of religious belief, as in that of political organization, the Malay state as a rule lacked the resources necessary for centralization of authority."

Although the British were technically only "advisers" in Malaya, with sovereignty continuing to be vested in the Malay sultans, the treaty arrangements they made left the traditional rulers without power to declare war, levy taxes, own slaves, or basically do "[any]thing that counted" (Yeger 1979, 91). Under the British the sultans became ceremonial heads of state. There was, however, one exception to this near-total control. Under the 1874 Pangkor Engagement with the State of Perak, which became a model for British control of all the Malay states, questions touching upon Malay religion and custom were "explicitly excluded from compulsory Residential 'advice'" (Roff 1967, 70). Denied substantive political authority, the sultans not surprisingly turned their attention to issues of faith. As Roff (ibid., 72) has argued, this preservation and strengthening of the traditional basis of authority of the sultans in the realm of "Malay religion and custom," combined with the centralized administrative power of British rule, produced "an authoritarian form of religious administration much beyond anything known to the peninsula before." Thus strengthened by the administrative machinery of the British, the Malay states were given extensive new powers for governing the practice of Islam. Laws passed after independence reinforced the arrangements of British colonial rule. Each state had an appointed religious council, which was empowered to regulate Muslim affairs. State departments of religion were given responsibility for managing day-to-day administration of Islamic matters and the "putative right to determine and convey what it meant to be a good and sufficient Muslim" (Roff 2009, 113).

This kind of power was not to go uncontested, and today PAS competes with the United Malays National Organization not only for the allegiance of the Malay majority but also for the not-inconsiderable patronage that comes with control of these state institutions. Moreover, because "management of religion is less a question of theology than part of a drive to maintain political control of the Malays," political competition tends to center on which party is more religiously correct and has the greater moral authority (Nagota 2010, 27). Faced with competition from PAS, which claims to promote Malay interests within the context of an Islamic state, UMNO has both tightened and centralized its control, federalizing a number of Islamic institutions. "These and similar measures, together with a tightening of prohibitory legislation affecting Muslims concerning, for example, public breaches of the Ramadan fast, served both to evidence government concern for acceptable Islamization and to emphasize its own zeal in Islamic causes" (Roff 2009, 107).

As important as the Muslim Brotherhood was in providing PAS with a political ideology and structure, the 1979 Iranian revolution may have been even more significant, leading in large part to the party's institutionalization of ulama rule in 1982 (Osman 2011, 43). Making the "hitherto romanticized idea of clerical leadership a reality," the Iranian revolution inspired both a revival of piety and new models of leadership (Liow 2011, 679). Most Malays have traditionally regarded religious scholars as "the legitimate authority to speak on behalf of the community on matters pertaining to Islam" (Saat 2012, 136). Some ulama gain formal legitimacy through the state, and others obtain popular legitimacy through their own credentials of piety, charisma, and family lineage. An example of the latter would be Nik Aziz Nik Mat (1931–2015), the highly regarded former chief minister of Kelantan and Murshidul Am (spiritual leader) of PAS.

Within PAS the vanguard of the movement for Islamic rule could be found in the youth wing. Liow (2011, 679) has noted: "After the Iranian revolution, the youth wing of PAS regularly dispatched senior members and leaders to Iran to interact with the government in Tehran, as well as to learn how the concept of *ulama* rule was being operationalized and implemented." These delegates included Subky Latif, one of *Harakah*'s founding editors, and future *Harakah* director general Mustafa Ali. Subky Latif remembers how impressed he had been by the stamina of the Iranians in the war with Iraq, and attributed this to ulama rule. "So I asked people there, what is the secret?" he said. "First, they have ulama leadership. And people listen to ulama. So I thought that PAS had to pioneer the concept of ulama leadership."

In 1982 the young reformers succeeded in forcing the party president to resign. Yusof Rawa, the former Malaysian ambassador to Iraq, became the new president, and the era of ulama leadership began. As in all things with PAS, however, the party "swung to the left or the right on various religious issues as the political landscape demanded" (Hwang 2010, 641), and by the 1990s some party leaders began to see the advantages of showing a friendlier and more tolerant face and aligning PAS with other opposition parties. The efforts of these "professionals" peaked in the 1998 Barisan Alternatif coalition, formed after the sacking of Deputy Prime Minister Anwar Ibrahim and the 2008 Pakatan Rakyat, which made unprecedented parliamentary gains and deprived Barisan Nasional of its traditional two-thirds majority.

Another influence in these alliances has been the victory of the Justice and Development Party (Adalet ve Kalkınma Partisi, AKP) in Turkey. When PAS leaders consulted with their counterparts from the AKP, they were advised to "end the use of threatening rhetoric, to de-emphasize the Islamic state, and to focus instead on issues such as the economy and corruption" (Hwang 2010, 648). Not insignificantly, those party leaders pushing for enhanced cooperation with other parties are often called the "Erdogan" faction. It is important to note that such cooperation did not eliminate the goal of the Islamic state but instead postponed it. As former *Harakah* editor Zulkifli Sulong explained in 2013, for PAS, "for every real Muslim" in fact, the Islamic state "is in our hearts." Yet this doesn't mean that PAS can't cooperate with others. Citing the fact that PAS has non-Muslim supporters, Zulkifli Sulong said:

> For me as a Muslim, we have to follow the Qur'an. To follow the Islamic
> rules. And we believe that the Islamic rules are the best. We can
> solve everything through Islamic teaching; that is the principle. When
> we compare PAS to UMNO, for example, [UMNO thinks] mostly of the
> cause of Malays. What happens to our neighbor who is not Malay, what
> happens to our friend who is not Malay? So we believe that Islam can give a
> better solution and a better system to Malaysia. That is why we support PAS.
> We believe that PAS, as an Islamic party, can bring a better way of life for
> everybody, not only for the Muslims. Because the rule has come from God,
> and God created us, and God knows our needs.

Tensions between the three parties making up Pakatan Rakyat came to a head after the 2013 general election, with Hudud becoming a key issue when PAS party president Hadi Awang tabled a Private Members Bill in Parliament to put the state of Kelantan's Hudud law into motion and did so without consulting Pakatan's leadership council.[1] With Anwar Ibrahim, the charismatic president of PKR (Pakatan Rakyat, the opposition coalition) imprisoned for the second time on sodomy charges, there was no one who seemed capable of healing the rift between the largely Chinese-Malaysian DAP and PAS.

At the 2015 *muktamar* (annual meeting), PAS swung again to the right, in what *Malaysiakini* called a "clean sweep" for the ulama leadership, "winning nearly all the central committee seats, while taking complete control of

PAS Youth and Muslimat [women's] wings." Incumbent president Hadi Awang crushed his challenger, securing 80 percent of the 1,160 votes cast.[2] It was a clear defeat for the professionals or "Erdogan" faction. Although there were many factors leading to this rout of the progressives, one that cannot be ignored was the role played by the largely Chinese-Malaysian DAP in its attempt to sway the convention outcome. As political analyst Bridget Welsh (2015) has noted, these interventions "hurt the progressive faction, with those seen as close to DAP . . . most affected." As she concluded, "the more the DAP leaders made statements about PAS leaders, the more they negatively impacted the faction they aimed to empower." According to former *Harakah Daily.net* editor Zulkifli Sulong, "about 80–90 percent" of *Harakah* journalists belong to the Erdogan faction."

OVERVIEW OF HARAKAH

Harakah's building is in an older part of Kuala Lumpur, in a shopping center not far from the Titiwangsa LRT stop, and in July 2013, I waited there to meet Ahmad Lutfi Othman, who was then editor-in-chief of *Harakah*. The meeting room has one glass wall, a big table, and about ten red chairs. It smells faintly of room freshener. One wall features a framed issue of *Harakah*'s pull-out section Fikra (literally "thought" or "idea") with photos of party leaders Nik Aziz Nik Mat and Hadi Awang and headlines reading "Islam is the foundation of PAS's strength" and "Tyranny has not ended."[3] The room is shabby, with worn carpet and newspapers piled up in the center of the table. A white board takes up one end of the room, with the word "Harakah" in red letters. On Tuesday, the morning after deadline night, the office was quiet.

Lutfi arrives at about 11 a.m., wearing a purple shirt and walking with a cane. One of the reporters explained earlier that Lutfi had been up very late working the night before and that he wasn't well. Heart troubles, diabetes, kidney problems—they said that Lutfi had recently spent a lot of time in the hospital. Given all of this, I was surprised by his energy. About fifty years old, he has an easy laugh and eyes that twinkle behind silver-rimmed glasses. He was born into a family that was "all PAS," and everyone in his *kampung* belonged to the Islamic party. "If there were UMNO members, they didn't want to admit it," he says, laughing. "Since the time I was little, my family, my father, always emphasized the importance that as a Muslim person, in our entire life, Islam has to be followed. By our worship, our ritual, praying, fasting— even the issue of politics." In Malaysia there is only one Islamic party, so

Offices of *Harakah*. Photo by author.

even if its leaders were "not perfect," Lutfi believes that he had no choice but to follow it. "If there is only one Islamic party, and if there is a problem in that party, then it is my *jihad* to straighten it out from the inside," he says. "Freedom of the press, this is only one part of the larger struggle of Islam."

Many Malaysian Muslims share the mainstream Sunni view of not publicly opposing a Muslim ruler, even if he is unjust. The results can be seen in UMNO-affiliated news organizations such as *Utusan* or *Berita Harian*. As Lutfi later explained, "in Sunni Islam the view is often heard that we should be loyal to the government, like we are to God and the Prophet. So our government's interpretation is that loyalty to the government is the same as to

God and the Prophet! Or even that the government is implementing the will of God and the Prophet." Muslim journalists at such alternative publications as *Harakah* and *Malaysiakini* take a different view—one that is often associated with Shia political thought: that Muslims are obligated to point out injustice, even if it originates with those in power. Thus the different political traditions that journalists embrace coincide with the extent to which they profess or are seen to be aligned either with the mainstream Sunni tradition, minority Sunni view, or even Shia political thought—which has been declared deviant by Malaysian religious authorities. PAS leaders and *Harakah* reporters who are inclined to this "leftist/antiestablishment brand of Islam" have been branded "Shia"—a label usually associated with victimhood, the ideology of protest, and resistance against entrenched or established power.[4] "I don't see Islam as opposed to press freedom," Lutfi concludes. "Because for me, the issue of responsibility, the issue of assertiveness, of justice itself—these are the bases of Islam that have been passed down. Opposing tyranny, defending those who are oppressed, this is the true mission of Islamic freedom."

Officially the newsletter of PAS, *Harakah* has a print edition that reached 130,000 people twice a week during the 2013 general election. The paper's online edition ranks number sixty among all websites accessed in Malaysia. Although the editors of *Harakah* and *HarakahDaily.net* struggle to reconcile the principles of journalism with both the teachings of Islam and the party's needs, they frequently run afoul of party leaders, who see the publications as vehicles for their own political ambitions. *Harakah's* editors are responsible to a board of directors consisting of ten party officials, one of whom is assigned to sit in on editorial meetings. *Harakah* was founded in 1986 and received its permit a few months later in 1987. As media scholar Cherian George (2006, 149) has demonstrated, its position as an overtly partisan organ makes it unusual in modern journalism as well as in Malaysia, where "independence" is a commonly expressed news norm. There is of course considerable irony to this, as all mainstream news organizations in Malaysia are owned by those who are close to one faction or another of the ruling coalition.

One of the founding editors of *Harakah* was Subky Latif, a former journalist from the newspaper *Utusan Malaysia*. He says he joined PAS in 1978, after the party was defeated in Kelantan. Now in his mid-seventies, Subky remains fiercely devoted to PAS, despite the recent upheaval in the party. "I felt that democracy had died when Barisan Nasional triumphed," he said. "So

Former *Harakah* editor Ahmad Lutfi Othman, 2015. Photo courtesy of Wira Andika Bin A. Halim.

I felt that I had a responsibility to guard this democracy, and I joined PAS. I entered two weeks after PAS was defeated. Not at a time when the party won, but when it lost." Subky was the only trained journalist who worked for *Harakah* full time. He recruited young PAS supporters from around Malaysia, including both Zulkifli Sulong from Terangganu and Ahmad Lutfi Othman from Kedah. The training lasted for two weeks. As there was no money for the candidate reporters, they were paid with food. One of the biggest challenges was determining what "Islamic journalism" would look like. Subky said he first thought about this at the inaugural international media conference of the Saudi-funded Muslim World League held in Jakarta in 1980.

Recalling that Indonesian vice president Adam Malik had opened the conference, Subky remembered that there had been discussion of how "in the world today, there is the American free press, and there is the controlled press in the Communist Bloc. But there is no Islamic press. So what if we could make an Islamic press as a result of this conference? But I thought that there was no one who knew what an Islamic press was." Unaware of any existing guidelines for Islamic journalism, Subky Latif drew up some of his own. First, as he told his young recruits, the Islamic press had to do what the Western press did—inform, entertain, educate, and criticize—but it had one further obligation: *dakwah*, or the propagation of the Islamic faith. "In information there is *dakwah*," he said. "In education, there must be *dakwah*. Even in entertainment, there can be *dakwah*."

"What about the need to criticize?" I asked. "Was that important in the Islamic press?" Subky answered firmly. "Yes. Even if you have 100 percent Islam, you still need criticism."

REFORMASI AND *REFORMASI*

As *Harakah* grew in circulation and prestige, the government responded by restricting its ability to publish. Although *Harakah* first appeared as a weekly, it soon went biweekly. During these early days, both Zulkifli Sulong and Ahmad Lutfi Othman recall having been inspired by events in Indonesia. When Lutfi left *Harakah* in 1998 to establish his own magazine, he named it *Detik* after the Indonesian magazine that had been banned in June 1994 along with *Tempo* and *Editor*. When Lutfi founded *Detik*, he took with him Fathi Aris Omar, a young Malaysian journalist who had been an occasional writer for *Harakah*. Although Lutfi and Fathi's careers eventually diverged (Lutfi stayed with PAS, while Fathi questioned the party and then went on to become a top editor at the independent news portal *Malaysiakini*), they remained firm friends. According to Fathi, Ahmad Lutfi Othman is one of the best editors and political commentators in Malaysia, although he is virtually unknown to foreign correspondents because he doesn't write in English. "We are on the same path," Fathi concluded in 2013. "Perhaps [Lutfi] is taking a more Islamist direction; I take a more liberal one."

The connection with Indonesia was not accidental. Both Lutfi and Fathi recalled having been inspired by the student-led pro-democracy movement across the Straits of Malacca that was known as *reformasi*. Along with Fathi, Lutfi helped to organize a program at the University of Malaya that featured leading Indonesian opposition figure Amien Rais. "I had a political connection with *reformasi*," he recalled, "but only via enthusiasm." Fathi's recollections are similar:

Lutfi was very moved with the student movement's success in toppling Soeharto. We monitored it from the very beginning. So when Amien Rais came over, we took Lutfi's motorbike, a very poor, very old motorbike from the *Harakah* office that night. We were very poor then, [the bike] was worse than the one used by the *Malaysiakini* team! It was one or two months after the downfall of Soeharto, and one or two months before Anwar was sacked from the government. So the spirit of protest and everything because of the economic crisis was the same, everything was there, and we were also hoping that one day we would have an uprising.

Lutfi said that he admired Indonesian leaders like Amien Rais and the Shiite intellectual Jalaludin Rahmat not only because of the way in which they spoke about social and economic problems but also because of the Islamic solutions they proposed. "I was always interested in people who could put out their ideas in shape in writing," he said, "and in Indonesia there were many figures that could do this." When Lutfi returned to *Harakah* after *Detik* was banned in 1999, he continued to call his weekly column "Catatan Hujung" (End Notes) in homage to founding *Tempo* editor Goenawan Mohamad and his famous column "Catatan Pinggir" (Side Notes).

On the eve of the 1999 general election and in the wake of Anwar Ibrahim's 1998 arrest and conviction, *Harakah*'s circulation numbers surged to 380,000. Once the election was over, the Mahathir government struck back at *Harakah*, restricting the paper's sales and circulation to PAS members only. When *Harakah*'s publication license expired in 2000, its new license allowed it to come out only twice monthly rather than twice weekly. Both of these restrictions were serious blows to the paper. Harassment from the Home Ministry would become a regular thing. Former editor Zulkifli Sulong described it as a cat-and-mouse game. Rosli Yaakop, *Harakah*'s managing director, was more blunt: "I would say that over the last twenty-seven years, the biggest challenge we have faced is harassment by the agents of the ministry of internal affairs. They confiscated our papers. Sometimes they took it down from the truck, or confiscated the papers from our distributors. And some of the distributors, they give up, they say, 'We don't want to sell your paper anymore, being constantly harassed, and we lost money as well when they took away our papers.' But this is a challenge, and we know that we've got to live with it."

There are different schools of thought not only as to what *Harakah* should cover but also to whom it should be sold. For Rosli, it's obvious that if you reach nonparty members, you can increase both sales and profits. A problem, however, is the Home Ministry, which restricts sales to party members.[5] Rosli explained:

> *Harakah*, of course, is the voice of the party. And this is the only channel of information for the members, and we have to really put it to maximum use so that we can disseminate information about the party activities, speeches of our leaders, our thinking about issues—these must go to the members especially. But Alhamdulillah, nonmembers also are buying it, reading it, so this is an additional bonus. But because our paper is restricted by the ministry of internal affairs, we have to write on the front page "for members only." So we are not as free as many other papers in terms of distributing our papers to the public.

It was partly as a result of these restrictions that in 2000 *Harakah* jump-started a dormant online edition that had been used as a tool during the 1999 general election. The editor was Zulkifli Sulong, who had been with the paper since the very beginning and became its chief editor in 1997.[6] With a tiny but devoted staff, Zulkifli made *HarakahDaily.net* into one of Malaysia's most-read online news sources. His commitment to independent media is as firm as his commitment to PAS—and even after he left *HarakahDaily.net* in 2013, he insisted that if the Islamic party were ever to come to power, it would remove all existing restrictions on the press with the exception of such things as pornography.

During the late 1990s one of the most interesting parts of *Harakah* was the English section, which was founded in 1996 and edited by Koya Kutty. Not a translation of the Malay section but rather a section in its own right, it featured articles by a wide range of scholars and writers, including non-Muslims. Today Koya Kutty is in his eighties, tall, and with a fierce look that belies his kindness and generosity. The proprietor of an Islamic publishing company, Koya Kutty is the father of six sons and daughters who hold a remarkable range of political views, including Latheefa Koya (a lawyer for Anwar Ibrahim's Keadilan party), Zakiah Koya (a highly regarded journalist and editor), and Abdar Rahman Koya (a columnist and writer who also works for his father's publishing house). Because he is always giving away books, Koya Kutty's children often despair of their father's publishing house ever making any money.

Sharing many of his father's views, Abdar Rahman Koya, who until a few years ago edited the paper's English section, noted that the problem with

Haji Koya Kutty with his grandchildren during the 2016 solar eclipse. Photo courtesy of Zakiah Koya.

Malaysia is that race is always mixed with religion. "So what I try to do," he said, "is to challenge some of this. We have too many right wing groups here under the name of Islam, and it is a very bad mix between racism and religious conservatism." While hardly liberal in perspective, both Abdar Rahman and his father use their knowledge of Islam to criticize what they regard as "narrow" views among the Malaysian ulama, including those in PAS. Abdar Rahman Koya has noted:

> *Harakah* is really conservative, not because of the journalism maybe but because of the people who are controlling it and the audience that is reading it, especially in the Malay section . . . and they are getting stronger and more vocal. Maybe they are small, but they are quite noisy. And because they can quote the Qur'an and the Hadith and all that, they try to portray themselves as more Islamic. And people say, "I won't argue with that, it's Islam."

So this shows how isolated we are in that debate. We are sidelining all the other scholars. If you look at our bookshops, you can see the kind of Malay Islamic books that they sell, they still sell the same old thing—the same old Hadith *tafsir* [interpretation], the same old Qur'anic exegesis. There is no fresh interpretation of the Qur'an. So that's why I was thinking that if they were to see the wide range of Islamic scholarship that is published in the West in English, they would be amazed. And none of them are liberal Islam. They are all practicing Muslims. So this is my complaint.

Kutty Koya's views were similar, and he resigned from *Harakah* in 2002 as a result of the uproar over an editorial he wrote stating that ulama were not infallible and that their judgments could be criticized. Under his editorship the English section published work by non-Muslims, such as the famed freelance journalist M. G. G. Pillai, and Raja Petra Kamarudin, the former director of the Free Anwar Campaign (George 2006, 145).

As editors of party organs, both Zulkifly Sulong and Ahmad Lutfi Othman were bound by party decisions on issues ranging from the implementation of Hudud to the goal of establishing an Islamic state. Although there are of course a range of opinions within the party, as an organization it is run by *shura* (decisions made by the group as a whole). As one of the writers for *HarakahDaily.net* explained (without irony), "there is no independent thinking in PAS." The challenges faced by these two editors were enormous. In 2012 the news organization was "reprimanded" by the party's youth wing at its annual *muktamar* (general meeting).[7] Claiming that the paper had sidelined party conservatives and promoted more liberal points of view, members passed a resolution demanding that the party "restructure the editorial makeup of *Harakah* so that it can interpret the true aspirations of PAS." Other contentious issues included whether to give space to the party's allies in Pakatan Rakyat, the alliance that consisted of Anwar Ibrahim's Justice Party (Partai Keadilan, PK) as well as the largely secular Democratic Action Party. Photos of Anwar Ibrahim and other opposition notables such as Penang chief minister Lim Guan Eng rankled with some PAS party members, who felt that the paper should focus exclusively on them.

When I suggested that maybe part of Lutfi's role at *Harakah* had been to educate PAS leadership about the importance of independent media, he laughed. "As ordinary human beings, ordinary politicians, it's difficult for them to hear criticism," he said. Yet Lutfi was quick to explain why some PAS politicians were frustrated with *Harakah* and wanted it to focus less on Pakatan Rakyat and more on the party itself. "In Malaysia," he said, "where there is no media freedom, and where the ruling parties have many outlets but PAS has only one, there is a sense of 'Why do we have to give space to material that can quote unquote hurt us?' I can understand that. I try to understand their concerns, and I think they also try to understand what I struggle for."

Not only do *Harakah*'s editors have to reconcile the needs of the party with their own sense of journalistic professionalism, but they also hold themselves to the higher standards of Islamic journalism. This comes out in *Harakah*'s view of verification that parallels *isnad* (the process of verifying the transmission of reports of the Prophet's words and actions). Zulkifli Sulong explained the relationship between verification and *isnad* this way:

> In Islam there are the Hadith, the sayings of the Prophet Muhammad. And they were written years and years later. The Prophet wasn't there but the scholars had to write them exactly as he said them. So how could they check it? *Isnad.* Person by person by person to the Prophet. Take Imam Bukhari, for example. He had to go one thousand miles to make it authoritative. A got it from B, B got it from C, C got it from D. And D? The Prophet Muhammad. It is like our concept of a journalist! We have to verify the news, find out whether it is true or not. That is the first principle. I always tell my friends, my colleagues, my journalists here, I say, "Truth. The story must be true. That's the first principle."

With a mixture of pride and ruefulness, Zulkifli pointed out that *Harakah* cannot attack "personalities" either. When asked about the mainstream media's focus on Anwar's "sex tape," he said: "When UMNO attacks Anwar Ibrahim as the head of PKR [Pakatan Rakyat, the opposition alliance], PKR always tends to revenge. 'Attack Najib, attack Rosmah!' But in *Harakah*, we cannot do that. We cannot do that; we won't do that! Because with PAS, no, you are meeting the ethics of Islamic journalism. You cannot judge a person without proof. We cannot publish that kind of story."

Ahmad Lutfi Othman, the newspaper editor, said something similar. "We are guided by the truth," he said. "This is always our aim. Our journalism is based on the Hadith that are given by the Prophet Muhammad. First, if there is any doubt at all about the truth of a story, however small, the story must be refused. And second, if a person comes bearing news, if it is felt that there is a problem with that person's character, especially if he is a trickster or a liar, then he must be refused. These are two teachings of the Prophet." For Lutfi, the "right of reply" is important within the context of justice, especially for opposition leaders like PAS politicians. Denied a place in the mainstream media, when they are criticized, they are never given space to answer. From this perspective, he noted, *Harakah* has to give them space. Finally, there is the issue of morality. "We aren't going to publish what we don't believe," he said. For example, in the world of entertainment, if there is a singer who appears with a group of Muslims, and she is not wearing a headscarf, "*Harakah* will give her one."

One of the most difficult aspects of *Harakah* is reporting on conflict within the party itself, or what *Harakah* managing director Rosli Yaakop referred to as "different, alternative opinions." Generally the paper waits until the party reaches a consensus and then reports on that. In Rosli's words: "This is something that I really appreciate in PAS. Everybody is allowed to express their opinion. But in the end the *shura*, the consensus, prevails. I have an opinion, the rest have their opinion, but we synthesize all the opinions, and the moment we reach a decision in the *shura*, that is it. And the rest of our opinions we must forget." He added that "in big issues, we must adhere to the *shura* decision, you know? Small issues, everyday life issues, we don't have to. But if the issue is really big and can get out of hand easily, we wait until the opinion of the *shura*."

Yet in an age of online news portals, social media, Twitter, Facebook, and blogs, and at a time in which most politicians have access to each of these, doesn't it seem somewhat naïve to assume that the news of "different alternative opinions" on big issues won't get out? This was certainly the view of the Malaysian language editors at *Malaysiakini*, who told me in 2014 that *Harakah* had made itself irrelevant. Today, they said, people use social media—especially Twitter—to find out what is *really* going on. So maybe there is no longer a need for *Harakah*. When *Harakah* can't report on controversy, they said, there are no sales. Former *HarakahDaily.net* editor Zulkifli Sulong said much the same thing: *Harakah*'s fate is tied up with that of PAS. When the people support PAS, he explained, they support *Harakah*:

During 1998, when Dr. Mahathir sacked Anwar Ibrahim, a lot of people come to PAS. And we at *Harakah*, we are quite open at that time. We reported what happened to Anwar, what happened to *reformasi*. And during that time, our *Harakah* is very very good. That's why [our circulation] goes to 380,000. *Harakah* will flourish when PAS is flourishing. When only PAS people buy *Harakah*, it is only 40,000 or 50,000. My idea for *Harakah* is always that we must not be the party newspaper, we must be the alternative newspaper. We must report the things that are not in the mainstream media.

So during the *reformasi* time, we find that when we publish Anwar's activities, Anwar's picture, the number of papers returned [from the distributors] will be very small. All sold out. So we make a decision in the editorial meeting that our party activities, yes, maybe at the back page, in the inside. We publish also, but not at the front page, the front page is so that the people will buy. After they've got our paper, they also read at the front page, but when they go inside, there's our party! Our news! If they didn't buy the paper, then how can we reach out to the people?

Agreeing with Zulkifli Sulong is Dr. Dzulkefli Ahmad, a former MP and director of PAS who has now joined the new Islamic party Amanah as the director of strategy. "Sales dwindled significantly," he said. "Readers and buyers are made up of [PAS] members, well-wishers, and as soon as they observe[ed] this kind of conflict and internal turbulence, I think they wanted to give a clear message to the management and to the party: 'If you people aren't going to put it right, we are just going to refuse buying.'"

Despite their commitment to Islam, PAS, and the Islamic movement, both Zulkifly Sulong and Ahmad Lutfi Othman sometimes chafed under the restrictions of the party. While matter-of-factly referring to their publications as "party organs," both editors acknowledged that they lacked the freedom of their counterparts at other media. By his own count, Lutfi has "entered and left *Harakah* maybe four times." He explained in 2013: "Among the reasons I left *Harakah*, there was a feeling of dissatisfaction with issues connected with media freedom. Not that *Harakah* was shackling me, not at all, but *Harakah* as a party organ has many regulations, guidelines, and I as a journalist-cum-publisher, I wanted to own my own company that could be more free."

But each time he left, Lutfi said, his connection with *Harakah* was still "intimate," and he always came back. "Although PAS leaders understand that I am Lutfi, who sometimes argues, sometimes complains," he said, "if

they are in a situation in which it is necessary, I am still available as a choice."
Lutfi continued: "They don't think, 'Oh this is Ahmad Lutfi who cannot be
controlled.'" After a laugh, he said, "All of the leaders of PAS still give me
room, as long as I don't do anything that would hurt the party." He said, "I
continue to feel that although there are sometimes big problems within the
party, between religion, politics, press freedom—I see this as a process. And
as a Muslim, I am certain that each process, or even each problem that I face,
is going to be evaluated by God as a sign of piety. Therefore this becomes a
motivation for me."

ISLAM AND FREEDOM OF EXPRESSION IN *HARAKAH*
AND THE PARTI ISLAM SE-MALAYSIA

Just how compatible are Islam and freedom of expression? Dzulkefli Ahmad,
who describes himself as an "Islamist Democrat" and is one of Malaysia's
leading progressive Islamic politicians and intellectuals, has argued that "the
principle of freedom in the sense of expression and conviction is very much
celebrated in Islam." He said:

> It is Islam that has got its tradition well-rooted in managing dissent,
> legitimate dissent or dissent by way of intellectual dissent and managing
> plurality if not outright pluralism. One of the characteristics of the
> believers as is mentioned in the Qur'an is that when God said, 'Glad tidings
> to those believers who are willing to listen to the speeches of man,' and
> [they are] able to sift through it all and follow what is better. To me, this is
> the most outstanding, the most illustrious verse that speaks for what should
> be the character of a believer. He is always willing to engage. He is always
> exposing himself to all kinds of opinions and convictions, yet at the end of
> the day he sifts through all of this and makes a judgment. . . . And to me
> journalism should also provide that space, that public space, for enhancing
> these conversations, this dialogue, this discourse, and, at the end of the day,
> allow for people to make a judgment out of all of this free enterprise of
> ideas, for them to come to their own conviction and conclusion.

Despite this commitment to freedom of expression, both PAS and everyone
connected with *Harakah* remains committed to idea of the Islamic state. As
Dzulkefli explained: "When you see yourself as an Islamist democrat, with
all of your advocacy, you are engaged in this contestation of ideas. So you get

to be voted in not because you are Islamist, or because your ideas are from God, you get to be voted in because of the efficacy of your ideas and your policies and programs. That makes us democrats."

Not everyone in PAS agrees with such a view, and certainly not everyone agrees that this should be the role of *Harakah*. One of the obstacles that *Harakah* journalists have to face is the idea that only the ulama are qualified to speak about Islam. Although the background to this is complex, and is related both to Malaya's colonial history and the state's role in regulating Islam (Steele 2014), it has significant implications for journalists, especially at a time when Malaysia's Islamic party is divided into two factions. So is it possible to be a good journalist and also to work for a party paper? For nearly thirty years, journalists and editors at *Harakah* have tried to do this. Sadly, it seems to have been an experiment that failed, and the "professionals" have either left *Harakah* or been sidelined. Yet Zulkifli Sulong, who remains a member of PAS, is convinced that there is room for freedom of expression in Islam. "I do not know how to quote the verses, how to quote the *Hadith*, but I know that [freedom of expression] is there," he said in 2014. "I do not know how to quote, because I am not in that field. But I know that I am right—for Malaysia, for the people, for my religion."

EPILOGUE

December 22, 2015, Kuala Lumpur. "Assalumalailkum," Azam calls into the dark house. There is no answer, and he calls out a few more times. After several minutes, Lutfi greets us at the door. Looking very frail, he's wearing a faded sarong with a bright green T-shirt. I am visiting with Noor Azam Shairi, a senior news editor from privately owned Astro Awami TV. We sit on the three sofas in Lutfi's living room—a pile of books on one and a couple of gadgets on another. A tablet lights up as new messages come in. Lutfi's daughter slips in with a plate of small cakes, cut up, a pot of tea, and three tea cups and saucers. Lutfi tells us that he has dialysis three times a week, for four hours a day, and that this will have to continue for the rest of his life.

I ask about *Harakah* and tell him that everyone I know from the paper has gone to a new website called *MalaysiaDateline*. He laughs and explains that the portal is owned by Amanah, the splinter party formed by the PAS members who were sidelined in the May 2015 muktamar (general meeting). Lutfi is still at *Harakah*, but he is no longer writing. He has been demoted from chief editor to the director of training. Although it is clear from his animated conversation with Noor Azam Shairi that he misses politics and still has plenty to say, he told me that if he were well enough to be writing, he wouldn't be writing for *Harakah*. "I no longer know PAS," he said.

Listening to Lutfi and Azam's animated conversation, from which Lutfi seems to draw energy, I think what a tragedy that these two gifted political observers and writers are not free to write what they really think—Lutfi because of illness, Azam because of ownership pressures and the self-censorship that stifle the Malaysian press. After we said our farewells to Lutfi, Azam and I continued our conversation in English on the LRT ride back to central Kuala Lumpur. I told him about my work and how difficult it is to find meaning in all of this. Is the point that an Islamic party cannot sustain independent media? No, he said, looking agitated. It's not the ideology, it's the party leaders. I looked at him quizzically. "They couldn't stand to be criticized," he added. I asked if he's saying that it's the politicians and not the party? "Yes. If they were true to Islamic principles, they would be humble, and accept criticism," he said. "They would be like Umar, the second Caliph, who said, 'I am no better than you, I am just doing what I have been asked. You must correct me if I do something that is wrong.'"

"And didn't he even accept criticism from a woman?" I asked, perhaps a bit too smugly.

Azam said yes, and we talked for a while about journalism and Islam. "It's like you said before," he said, "the principle of verification—*tabayyun*. When you see an unreliable person in the street, you must approach with caution." He added: "But this has been misused by Najib. He even quoted it in order to defend himself, basically telling UMNO members to be skeptical of media reports."[8] The prime minister's comment was about 1MDB—the corruption scandal that was initially reported in Western media.

"Even the devil can quote scriptures," I said.

"It's like this," Azam explained: "No politician likes to be criticized. PAS, Pakatan, even DAP. They are all the same. It's not the ideology, it's the political leaders."

"Maybe you're right," I said, feeling more cheerful. "It's not the ideology. There's nothing in Islam that prevents independent media." As Azam suggested, it is possible to justify journalists' critical attitudes and skepticism toward the truth of their own opinions either with liberal theory and the words of John Locke or with *tabayyun*. The principal is the same; it's the road that's different.

FOUR

MALAYSIAKINI

Islam in a Secular Context

WHY WOULD a member of United Malays National Organization (UMNO) and a self-described "religious conservative" want to work for *Malaysiakini*, an independent news portal known for its coverage of the opposition, relentless reporting on double standards among government-sponsored Islamic guardians of virtue, and promotion of debate and discussion on matters of controversy in Islam among Muslims? It might surprise *Malaysiakini*'s critics in the ruling coalition to learn that since its founding, there have been not one but several UMNO members working for the news organization that media scholar and critic Cherian George (2006) once called an example of "contentious journalism." Likewise, there are many pious Muslims at *Malaysiakini* who not only pray five times a day and fast during Ramadan but also think very deeply about journalism and Islam and how to reconcile the two.

Similar to *Harakah*, the newspaper of the opposition Pan-Malaysian Islamic Party (Parti Islam Se-Malaysia, PAS), the history of *Malaysiakini* is closely intertwined with that of *reformasi* (Chin 2003; Nain 2002)—the name for the loose coalition of pro-democracy actors who came together after the sacking of Deputy Prime Minister Anwar Ibrahim in 1998. But unlike *Harakah*, *Malaysiakini* is not affiliated with any political party or organization; its goal is independence. As CEO Premesh Chandran has explained: "At that time there were lots of *reformasi* websites, which were very, very pro-Anwar. We tried to explain that *Malaysiakini* is going to be a website, but it's not going to be *reformasi*, it's going to be independent news. And nobody gets it. They say, 'If you start a website, you guys are going to be seen like *reformasi*.'

Malaysiakini CEO Premesh Chandran, 2014. Photo courtesy of Nur Nadyatul Syima.

And we said no, we are going to have bylines; we are going to write in a professional way."

Launched in November 1999, *Malaysiakini* was created by Steven Gan and Premesh Chandran, two young journalists who got their start at the Kuala Lumpur newspaper *TheSun*. Believing that political control had corrupted the values of good journalism in the mainstream media, they wanted to bring independent news and in-depth analysis to the Internet. Using the norms of good journalism—covering both sides, providing supporting evidence, and giving voice to the voiceless—*Malaysiakini* legitimized alternative views of events and challenged the authoritarianism of the ruling coalition Barisan Nasional (Steele 2009). Thus *Malaysiakini*'s agenda was not "*reformasi*" in the narrow sense; it was much more than that.

Malaysiakini is multiethnic, multiracial, and multireligious. As editor-in-chief Steven Gan explained, from the beginning their goal was "to create an independent news organization that would open up the issues of press freedom and human rights, enhance democracy, and show people why these issues were so important." Gan continued:

> Prem and I wanted to project a Malaysian viewpoint, that whenever we write, we'll just discard who we are and look at it from a Malaysian perspective. Unlike perhaps the *New Straits Times*, which is UMNO-linked, and sees things from a Malay perspective, or the vernacular papers—they each have their own perspective: the Tamil papers, the Chinese papers, the Malay papers. And I think the other major thing is that we were trying to create a platform for all these different groups, to generate a discussion, a cross-racial, cross-cultural, cross-religious discussion. When you look at *Malaysiakini*, it would be what it should be if Malaysians didn't think about race.

Although Malay-Muslims make up slightly more than half of the population of Malaysia, there are also sizable non-Muslim populations, including Chinese and Indian minorities.[1] At the end of World War II, the British proposed to create a multiethnic and multiracial Malayan Union, in which all citizens would be granted equal status regardless of race or ethnicity. This plan was unacceptable to Malay elites, who successfully mobilized communal Malay sentiment against the British proposal and in favor of the ethnonationalist loyalty promoted by UMNO. The resulting 1957 constitution was designed to "safeguard the position of the traditional rulers as constitutional monarchs[,] create a common nationality for the Federation . . . and uphold the special position of the Malays" (Abbot and Franks 2007, 342). By granting the Malays "special privileges," the constitution thus "ensure[d] that ethnic and religious identification would remain the defining characteristic of social, economic and political discourse" (ibid., 342).

In many ways the current press situation in Malaysia resembles that of Indonesia under Soeharto, in that print publications are tightly controlled. The Malaysian constitution guarantees freedom of expression but allows a host of limitations on this right. Harsh criminal defamation laws are regularly used to impose restrictions on the press, and the 1948 Sedition Act, a relic of British colonial rule, criminalizes any act with "seditious tendency" that might "excite disaffection" or "bring into hatred or contempt" the rule of the government. The 1984 Printing Presses and Publications Act (PPPA) gives the government the authority to grant or deny license applications and revoke licenses at any time without judicial review. The Internet is the one bright spot in this otherwise gloomy landscape, with the government formally committed to a policy of refraining from direct online censorship. Web content, however, is monitored by the Malaysian Communications and Multimedia Commission (MCMC). Although the media industry is dominated by private ownership, the majority of print and broadcast outlets are controlled either by political parties in the ruling coalition or by businesses with political connections to the government. *Malaysiakini* is an exception to this rule (Steele 2009).

Although *Malaysiakini*'s English-language reports are behind a paywall, the news portal continues to rank number one among Malaysian news sites—despite having spawned a number of online imitators. In recent years it has reported extensively not only on the opposition but also on such issues as the billion-dollar 1Malaysia Development Berhad (1MDB) investment fund scandal, which suggests a mind-boggling level of political corruption directly connected to Prime Minister Najib Razak. Although the *Wall Street Journal* earned recognition as a Pulitzer Prize finalist for reporting that hundreds of millions of dollars from the government-backed fund were deposited in the prime minister's accounts to secure victory in the 2013 general election, these developments have received little coverage in Malaysia other than in online media.[2] Instead, the politically connected mainstream media publishes only the government's denials—along with its threats to sue or shut down its critics.

Malaysiakini's editorial desk has three news sections (English, Malay, and Chinese), which in 2016 consisted of forty-four people, and KiniTV, which employs another fourteen. Although there is some effort to balance the newsroom between Malaysia's three largest ethnic groups—Malay, Indian, and Chinese—what makes *Malaysiakini* different from other news organizations is not the diversity of the newsroom per se but rather the effort to deal directly with such sensitive issues as ethnicity, race, and religion, and to do so within an environment of mutual respect. As Gan said: "I think it is very difficult for Malaysians to think outside their own ethnic identification. . . . [It's apparent] when you fill out a form, in everything that you do. I know that people will argue that we shouldn't emphasize race in our reports, but if we try to report in a way that race doesn't matter, that is dishonest. Even when we hire people, we think about how we are going to attain a balance. It's a conscious effort."

Malaysiakini editor Steven Gan, 2014. Photo courtesy of Nur Nadyatul Syima.

Malaysiakini is not "Islamic." Gan keeps discussion of religion out of the newsroom and dislikes the use of the word "secular," which is problematic in an environment in which religion has been so politicized. Nevertheless, it is clear that the publication is nonconfessional. Although covering topics such as *murtad* (religious apostasy) can make people at *Malaysiakini* feel uncomfortable, they are nevertheless required to do it. Gan described a conversation he once had with a Malay reporter who preferred not to write about issues related to Islam, as he was afraid that his coverage would not be to the liking of *Malaysiakini*'s readers and thus not considered "objective." Gan recalled telling the reporter, "Look, you are a journalist. There is no way out. You have to do these stories."

RAMADAN, ISLAM, AND THE STATE

For the past several years, I have been in Malaysia and Indonesia during Ramadan, the month in which the Qur'an was revealed to the Prophet Mohammad. During Ramadan, Muslims refrain from eating, drinking, smoking, and sexual activity between first dawn and evening prayers. In 2010, when I was just beginning my research into journalism and Islam, I decided to join *Malaysiakini*'s Muslim journalists in fasting. I had often done this in Indonesia while doing research on *Tempo* magazine. There is far less evidence of fasting at *Malaysiakini* than there is at *Tempo*. Not all of the Muslim journalists fast, and although people don't eat or drink in front of those who do, life otherwise goes on pretty much as usual. Many expressed surprise that I intended to fast. One who was encouraging was Fauwaz Abdul Aziz, who was at that time an assistant news editor.

Fauwaz, the son of a diplomat, grew up overseas. A pious Muslim and then a degree candidate in the graduate program at the International Islamic University, Fauwaz held views on matters of Islam that were frequently sought out by his colleagues. Fauwaz said that during Ramadan the shops—even those run by Muslims—are still open during the day and serve non-Muslims. He pointed out that there is nothing in Islam that forbids Muslims from earning a living during Ramadan. Yet the government enforces fasting, and shop owners are forbidden to serve Muslims. "There will be raids," said Vicknésan Sampasivam, who is Indian-Malaysian and was one of *Malaysiakini*'s senior editors. "Not on a very large scale, but they will be highly publicized. All the papers will carry news of the raid, and I suppose even the charging in court."

After a few days of fasting and breaking the fast together with the Muslim journalists, I decided to stop. I sent an email to Fauwaz and others explaining that fasting was interfering with my ability to work. Although I had learned a lot from my experiment, I wrote, it was time to end it. Although what I had written was true, it was only part of the truth. It was clear to me that my fasting had become disruptive. Whereas in Indonesia, journalists at *Tempo* had embraced my interest in fasting, at *Malaysiakini* I felt that many of the Muslim journalists were at best baffled by my desire to join in and at worst somewhat offended. At *Tempo* the feeling had been "We believe that if you fast, you are honoring us." At *Malaysiakini*, however, the sense I received from Muslims and non-Muslims alike was that Ramadan is for Muslims and that a non-Muslim has no business fasting at all.

Why were my experiences in Malaysia so different from those in Indonesia? *Malaysiakini*'s newsroom, like *Tempo*'s, is a demonstrably pluralist place, embracing diversity and explicitly standing for religious tolerance. One explanation for the lack of enthusiasm may lie in the differing histories of

Indonesia and Malaysia. In Malaysia the state is involved in religious affairs to a degree that would be unimaginable in neighboring Indonesia (Bertrand 2010; Nagota 2010; Anwar 2001). This level of state involvement, in addition to the more recent politicization of Islam, has had profound implications for the ways that Muslims and non-Muslims interact even in otherwise pluralist spaces. In Indonesia I never encountered a Muslim journalist who was unwilling to talk about his or her view of religion and work. In Malaysia, however, a standard reply to my questions was something along the lines of "I'm not the right person to ask," or "I don't feel that I have the authority to comment." As Aidila Razak, a young, independently minded *Malaysiakini* journalist who earned her undergraduate degree in Australia, said wryly, in Malaysia "there's a state that's the expert." How did the state come to be seen as the "expert" on matters of religion in Malaysia? Historians and scholars of Islam point to the legacy of British colonialism, which strengthened and even institutionalized the relationship between Islam and the state.

As I noted in chapter 3, although the British were technically only "advisers" in Malaya, with sovereignty continuing to be vested in the Malay sultans, treaty arrangements left the traditional rulers without power and as little more than ceremonial heads of state. The one exception was in the realm of Malay religion and custom, which by law was Islamic. Strengthened by the administrative machinery of the British, the Malay states were given extensive powers for governing the practice, beliefs, and doctrines of Islam. Laws passed after independence reinforced these arrangements. Each state has an appointed religious council, which is empowered to regulate Muslim affairs. State departments of religion were given responsibility for managing day-to-day administration of Islamic matters as well as the "putative right to determine and convey what it meant to be a good and sufficient Muslim" (Roff 2009, 103).

Whether most Malaysians are aware of this history, they are acutely aware of the states' power to regulate Muslim affairs and to determine who is and who is not a good Muslim. In the words of Aidila Razak, "the reason why people say, 'Oh, I'm not an expert' goes back to the fact that there's one Islam and nothing else is accepted. So because of that, it is sensitive, because you're so scared to say something wrong." Shufiyan Shukur, who was at the time *Malaysiakini*'s senior video editor, agreed, saying that only the ulama are authorized to speak about religion: "So I cannot say something because I am not an ulama. You have to be approved. [Even] if you think you have gone through a religious education in the top university in India or Cairo, if you are not approved by this council of ulama and religious department, you cannot even teach religion."

In practical terms the control of all matters Islamic by the state has led to a situation in Malaysia in which ordinary Malays feel reluctant—if not powerless—to speak about religious matters, as there can be legal consequences to challenging the state's interpretation of Islam. At *Malaysiakini*, which is known for its agenda of human rights, freedom of expression, and ethnic and religious tolerance, Ramadan thus raised a number of difficulties, even in a space that is demonstrably pluralist in that all religions are afforded equal legitimacy.[3] It was clear that my decision to fast was problematic. As Vicknésan Sampasivam said: "I think for most Malaysians [fasting at Ramadan] is a religious ritual. They don't see it as having a social purpose, it is purely religious. You're well aware that there are religious divides in the country. And so the thing is, why would I want to partake? I'm a Hindu. If a Muslim comes up to me and says—and you know about Thaipusam festival, it's a body piercing—I want to do it, I would be very surprised! Why would you want to do that?"

Vicknésan suggested that perhaps the Muslims at *Malaysiakini* reacted the way they did because they were worried that I might be fasting "without understanding the whole picture." He asked, "Why would you want to do it if you're not ready to come into the religion?" For non-Muslims the situation was even more complicated. Again, in his view, "it never occurs to a non-Muslim, why don't I join my Muslim colleagues for fasting this month? We don't do it ourselves, so I suppose we wonder why would anyone else want to do it?" *Malaysiakini* video editor Shufiyan Shukur said much the same thing: "I think that for the Muslims, they think why put yourself through the torture that we have to undergo? And then for the non-Muslims, they are afraid that you will become a Muslim. [Laughs.] Which is a big deal."

Although it made them uncomfortable to say it, several non-Muslims at *Malaysiakini* noted that during Ramadan there was a clear distinction between the Muslims and the non-Muslims: "They fast and we don't fast." Or as Aidila Razak said, "Maybe at *Malaysiakini* to be Muslim is sometimes considered to be quite conservative, and it's not really the thing to do? It could be that. You don't want to make a fuss about it because then you pressure other people to do it." Ordinarily at *Malaysiakini* one doesn't wear one's religious identity on one's sleeve, but during Ramadan these distinctions are clear-cut. Again, quoting Aidila Razak:

> I thought about it, because yesterday I was with [a Chinese colleague] at the Sessions Court. So he asked me if I was going back to the office because it was 5:00 something or 6:00, and I said yeah, or I didn't know if I should just go back because there would be traffic jam blah blah blah, and then he said, "No no, you shouldn't just go back, I can go back. You shouldn't because you're fasting and I'm Chinese." It was really strange, he said, "I'm Chinese, therefore I can go back." He could be Chinese-Muslim. It's just the first time he said that to me—"I'm Chinese and you're Malay."

Several non-Muslims at *Malaysiakini* commented on how Ramadan posed unique problems for journalists. Not only does everything slow down during the fasting month, especially in government offices, but there is also a feeling of "tension." Former video editor Indrani Kopal commented:

> [Chief editor] Steven is more grumpy during Ramadan, that would be one thing. If you are fasting, you don't perform as well as you do when you're not fasting, so if the news is fast, quick, can you equally perform? Malaysians have this bad habit during Ramadan, saying that everything slows down. The whole system slows down. People go back early, the office closes, you call up somebody, and they say he's outside. You walk up to a shop that normally closes at 5:00 and it is closed because they are fasting. A lot of organizations, especially the government offices, they go home at 2:00, and they don't come back. The reason is "I'm fasting." A lot of people take advantage of this.

Although other *Malaysiakini* journalists disagreed with these sentiments, saying that life went on pretty much as usual, the tensions were nevertheless evident. As Hazlan Zakaria, a thoughtful writer and journalist in his thirties, noted, Muslims in Malaysia have been encouraged by the government to fear non-Muslims and vice versa: "Here, there is this feeling that the government is trying to orchestrate Muslims against non-Muslims and Malays against non-Malays, which is creating this kind of so-called invisible backlash."

As anthropologist Joel S. Kahn (2006, xii) has argued, at the time of independence, a single view of "Malayness" came to dominate Malaysia, and more cosmopolitan alternatives lost out. In the realm of religion this has come to mean, as Aidila Razak said, that "there is a right way and a wrong way to be a Muslim—and only one way to be right. And you're scared of the consequences of being wrong." Although "*Malaysiakini* is trying to present a pluralist alternative," Aidila said, "the state is saying, 'You must fast.'" Yet, she hastened to add, "It's still an individual choice." But how much of a choice is it, when there is also such "tremendous social pressure" and even harassment? Moreover, it is not only the Muslims who are scared of the consequences of being wrong. A senior Malaysian journalist who asked not to be named told me: "I'm willing to state my opinion, but I do not want to be named, because anything [I say about] about Islam can be misconstrued."

RAMADAN AND EVERYDAY RESISTANCE IN MALAYSIA

Not all of the Muslims at *Malaysiakini* fast. Those who do not fast have their own reasons, including health concerns or an inability to work. Those who do fast are decidedly nonjudgmental about their colleagues, pointing out that fasting should not continue if it interferes with doing one's job. Yet, interestingly, several journalists at *Malaysiakini* and elsewhere expressed a different reason for refusing to fast, which had more to do with the state than with issues of health or the ability to do one's work. If anything, what I observed resembled anthropologist James Scott's (1985, 29) definition of "everyday resistance," the "Brechtian forms of class struggle [that] require little or no coordination or planning . . . [and that] typically avoid any direct symbolic confrontation with authority or with elite norms." In the case of Ramadan in the newsroom, these "ordinary weapons" included buying food for those who weren't fasting, eating openly in front of others, and complaining about the hypocrisy of the state religious authorities.

Malaysiakini's Shufiyan Shukur suggested that hypocrisy rather than religion is the problem. If fasting during Ramadan is supposed to remind people of what it means to be poor and hungry, why are there such huge feasts in hotels? He went on to ask:

The thing is, does fasting make you a better person? It is supposed to let you
feel what it is like to be starving for so many hours in a day. But for those
who are poor, who are starving, who are living in poverty, they don't have

the luxury of at 7:30, here comes the *azan* [call to prayer], and wow, food is there! They don't have that. They are starving from morning to night, with maybe one or two meals a day for 365 days a year.

To the upper echelons of Malay society, this whole Ramadan is a big gig, a show. Because you know, every evening somewhere in the major hotels and restaurants of KL and everywhere in the country people [are] making plans to have a good meal, a good *buka puasa* with friends, family, and relatives. It goes on all the time. So this is why the restaurants and the hotels, they put up big huge buffets. And those who earn below subsistence, they don't get that.[4]

On August 19, 2010, journalist Deborah Loh wrote an article for the online publication *The Nut Graph* in which she addressed the problem of what she called "reciprocity in understanding." Titled "Why Fast during Ramadan If One Is Non-Muslim?," the article focused on two non-Muslims who fasted during the entire month. Both of these individuals said that they did it for "solidarity" and to better understand their Muslim friends. Yet Loh (2010) claimed she found this reason to be baffling:

> And yet, just what does "showing solidarity" mean in our context where Muslims and Malay Malaysians are the majority? And where non-Muslims have to abide, not by choice but by decree, to various directives such as a ban on new non-Muslim clubs in schools and a ban on using the word "Allah" when it isn't exclusive to Islam? Or where non-Muslims have no say in the unilateral conversion of children if one's spouse converts to Islam, and have to give up burial rights over a deceased Muslim family member's body? Why should solidarity be shown with the majority if such are the circumstances for the minority?

If we define pluralism as according legitimacy to different ways of being in the world, than it is hard to say that Malaysia—a country in which one group is accorded special privileges by the constitution—is truly pluralist. Even in spaces such as *Malaysiakini* that are avowedly pluralist in character, the state ideology has ways of influencing how people think about one another. Worse yet, the politicization of Islam and the maneuvering by political parties and groupings to outdo one another in displays of piety have had insidious effects on how people interact on a daily basis.

Malaysiakini journalists in their late forties and mid-fifties remember fondly a day in which race and religion were less politicized, and there was more possibility for real friendship among people of different religions and ethnicities. Shufiyan Shukur, who spent much of his youth in the United Kingdom and returned to Malaysia in the 1980s, recalled:

> Many years ago, I was invited to my friend's Chinese [new] year. Now I don't get invited anymore. Why? Because in '81 when I first came back, they would say, 'Okay, Shuf, this is pork. This is okay, this is chicken.' But the chicken would come from a Chinese grocer, in fact. But now even my friends are very concerned about it. If they were to invite me, it would have to be a special occasion when everything was halal, that kind of thing. Or they [would have to] take me to . . . a special lunch somewhere in a restaurant that's halal. But it didn't used to be like that. There's a lot of change. It's a change I don't like to see, but that's just the way it is.

Chief editor Steven Gan described a kind of social interaction that is now gone, replaced by a superficial state-sponsored "multiculturalism." In the old days, he said, race was not emphasized as much as it is today. Relationships were more natural, and "we thought less of ourselves as Chinese or Malay or whatever it is." He continued:

> It is different now. And it is impeding all sorts of relationships, even friendships. I live in a housing estate that is almost 95 percent Malay, and the Chinese there are pushed more or less unconsciously into a ghetto, and also I think that there is among the Malays a greater consciousness of Islam. And that has also helped to increase the gap. . . . And the open houses—again the Chinese are unsure about inviting the Malays into their house because you do not know exactly whether things are halal, and you are not so confident about that, and Malays are also uneasy about going because they feel it may be impolite to reject certain things. So it is not natural. It becomes more difficult in that sense.

RECONCILING FAITH WITH WORK

It is not only Ramadan that brings to the forefront potential conflicts between faith and work; many of the daily activities of journalism raise questions that trouble some of the more pious Muslims at *Malaysiakini*. Perhaps most problematic for Muslim journalists are Islam's strict prohibitions against gossip, libel, and other forms of defamation. According to Indonesian Islamic university lecturer Faris Khairul Anam (2009), reports of sexual impropriety may not be published until they have been proven in a court of law—even if a confession has been made in front of a journalist. Exposing something shameful about another person is also forbidden, as is backbiting. *Malaysiakini* journalist Hazlan Zakaria explained:

> In Islam there are certain things that you are not supposed to report even if
> they are true. Because one, you are not supposed to debase your fellow
> Muslims. If you know they have done something wrong, you can tell
> them . . . but you are not supposed to announce it to the public. You don't
> shame your brothers and sisters. And second, the standards that you need
> to prove something is true in Islam are far higher than in legal terms in
> Western or Roman or British law. And that is a problem, because most of
> the things we can report and get away with legally, actually goes against
> Islamic law, because the acid test in Islamic law is very high.

The question of when a Muslim journalist can properly divulge something negative about someone else has implications not only for the popular understanding of libel and defamation but also for investigative reporting. What are the limits to reporting about charges that have not yet been proven in court? How do journalists understand the nature of watchdog journalism (Waisbord 2000) or investigative reporting, which generally starts with an assumption that either something (or someone) isn't working in the way it is supposed to?[5] As media scholars James Ettema and Theodore Glasser (1998, 34) have pointed out, one of the most common "master frames of investigation" is "the demonstration of a pattern of harm or wrong doing, followed by an explanation of how a system or institution has failed."

Under Malaysia's system of "electoral authoritarianism" (Case 2011), in which the ruling Barisan National (National Front) coalition controls all mainstream press outlets (Gomez 2004; George 2006; Abbot 2011), accusations of "trial by the media" are frequently voiced by opposition figures and civil society members who are critical of the ruling parties. In a system that is markedly "not free," news organizations generally operate in the interests of political actors. Despite familiar injunctions against "trial by the media," the Malaysian press is filled with examples of gossip and backbiting, both of which are explicitly forbidden in Islam. At *Malaysiakini*, concern with politically motivated news—and the profusion of "sex videos"—has led to much discussion of journalism ethics and efforts to elevate the quality of reporting. Former *Malaysiakini* journalist Fauwaz Abdul Aziz explained how difficult it was to reconcile his faith with the daily work of journalism in Malaysia:

> There are certain things you do as a journalist that don't exactly jibe with what a religious person can or cannot, should or should not be doing. Say that somebody is accused of a sexual impropriety. You don't even mention that act of impropriety unless you have concrete proof. In religion this would be so grave that in an Islamic state, or during the time of the Prophet, you would be guilty of falsely accusing somebody. There are punishments in the Qur'an, corporal punishment. And all of the people in that chain of disseminating [the false story] would be punished as well.

The teachings of Islam notwithstanding, Malaysian media gave considerable coverage to the sex video that emerged in March 2011 and purportedly contained images of former Malaysian deputy prime minister and opposition leader Anwar Ibrahim having sex with a prostitute. In his landmark study of American journalism, sociologist Herbert Gans (1979, 188–90) noted that American journalists generally do not focus on the implications of their work, pointing out that such a focus would lead to paralysis. In Indonesia and Malaysia, however, popular understanding of journalists' responsibility for the outcome of their work is different. Whether this is entirely because of Islam is unclear, although there appears to be a consensus that journalists should be attuned to the consequences of what they write. This focus on implications and outcomes may further be related to the popularity and persistence of the notion of "trial by the press." Two cases illustrate the particular challenges Muslim journalists face: the first example is the Anwar sex video; the second is the "shoe-throwing imam," whose one-year prison sentence for throwing his shoes at a Malaysian Federal Court judge prompted some soul-searching in at least one Malay journalist who reported on it for *Malaysiakini*.

THE ANWAR SEX VIDEO

On Monday, March 21, 2011, reporters from Malaysia's mainstream news organizations and leading online media received a mysterious telephone summons to Carcosa Seri Negara, a luxury hotel owned by the Malaysian government. As *Malaysiakini*'s Hazlan Zakaria reported, an unidentified female voice promised that he would be seeing something "huge and explosive."[6] The event turned out to be a special screening of a sex video, provided by a mysterious man who called himself Datuk T. The star of the video was a man whom *Malaysiakini* described as having "an uncanny likeness to a key opposition figure." Bloggers and pro-government social media weren't so coy, quickly asserting that the man *was* opposition leader and former deputy prime minister Anwar Ibrahim.

Although Anwar and other opposition politicians denounced the tape as doctored, the story was too delicious to ignore, and for days media coverage focused on the size of the man's belly, the identity of the mysterious Datuk T, and the question of (as Anwar's wife noted), "If Anwar was alleged to have affair[s] with men, why is there a video showing him with a woman?"[7] Within a week, it became clear that "Datuk T" was actually three men, each of whom had close ties to the United Malays National Organization (UMNO), the lead partner in the ruling National Front coalition. They were businessman Shazryl Eskay Abdullah, former Malacca chief minister Rahim Thamby Chik, and Shuib Lazim, the former treasurer-general of Perkasa, an organization devoted to Malay supremacy.[8] After what the opposition claimed was some foot-dragging by the police, the three men were charged with possession and distribution of pornography under Section 292(a) of the Penal Code. After pleading guilty, they were fined a total of MYR 5,500 or about US$1,720.[9]

It was never determined conclusively whether the man in the video was Anwar Ibrahim, but the incident kept discussion of the opposition leader's sexual proclivities in the public arena for several months, as the country underwent important elections in Sarawak and Anwar awaited the verdict in what was widely seen as a politically motivated trial for sodomy. In an interview with *Malaysiakini*, Wan Azizah, Anwar Ibrahim's wife and the president of Partai Keadilan, referred explicitly to how media reports on the incident had violated the fundamental teachings of Islam: "For us Muslims we believe *fitnah* (slander) is a big sin. Not only do you get punished but your children and the generation beyond that. . . . In Arabic, it is *aib* (disgrace) to your *maruah* (dignity), it's my husband you are talking about. It's the family's dignity. We are together (on this)." She concluded: "This is trial by the media."[10] On the surface the Anwar sex video appears clearly to violate the strictures against spreading gossip of a sexual nature. The fundamental question is why were Malaysian media so eager to report on it?

If in Malaysia news coverage of the Anwar sex video raised uncomfortable questions about "trial by the media," the story of the "shoe-throwing imam" caused at least one journalist at *Malaysiakini* to wonder about the consequences of media reports and what happens "when we report [things] . . . not because of any societal value, but purely because of the sensational value." The incident began on June 16, 2011, when an imam at the Ar Rahimah mosque in Kampung Pandan Kuala Lumpur was evicted from his home within the mosque grounds because of "disciplinary problems." The imam, Hoslan Hussain, said that he had been evicted for highlighting corruption and abuse of funds at the mosque. Claiming that he had made numerous reports to the Malaysian Anti-Corruption Commission and also to the police, the imam said that there had been no action. "In fact," he was quoted as saying, "Umno [United Malays National Organization, the lead partner in the ruling coalition] extends its powers on the mosque. It was Umno's hands behind this and it used MAIWP [Federal Territory Islamic Affairs Council] to remove me."[11]

The lawyers for the Islamic Affairs Council disputed this account, saying that the imam had refused to read the required Friday sermon and that there had been other complaints about him as well. When the imam appeared in Federal Court in February 2012, his appeal to have his case heard was denied—the Court apparently agreed with the objection of the Federal Territory Islamic Affairs Council that Hoslan's affidavit had been filed outside of the proper time frame. The imam, who represented himself, was frustrated with the ruling. After a brief argument, he took off one of his shoes and threw it at the bench. When the shoe missed the judge, the imam took off his other shoe and threw it as well, hitting the deputy registrar of the apex court. As *Malaysiakini* reported, "the three-member bench did not initiate any contempt order against Hoslan," but "the deputy registrar is said to have asked mainstream media not to report the shoe throwing."[12]

The first story in *Malaysiakini* that appeared on February 22, 2012, prompted sixty-four comments from subscribers—all but five supporting the imam if not his actions per se. The reasons for this were clear, as a brief section near the bottom of the story stated:

Hoslan also admitted to being a staunch supporter of the opposition, especially PAS [Parti Islam Se-Malaysia, or the Pan-Malaysian Islamic

Party], and said he helped out in every by-election campaign the party was involved in.

At the height of the Bersih 2.0 saga [a demonstration in support of electoral reform] last year, he said, the Friday sermon at his mosque advised the people not to attend the rally.

Upon hearing the sermon, Hoslan said, he lifted his robe in protest before the congregation, to show them his yellow Bersih T-shirt.[13]

As Hazlan Zakaria, the *Malaysiakini* reporter who wrote several follow-up stories on the shoe-throwing imam explained: "To put this in context, there have been cases of the BN [Barison Nasional or National Front]–controlled government sidelining, [putting into] cold storage, victimizing people who support the opposition in the Islamic authorities. Certain religious officials . . . have been fired just because they support the opposition. And this particular imam is very vocal in supporting the opposition, and he supports Bersih. So there are theories that he was victimized not because he exposed corruption, but because he was an opposition supporter." Hazlan added: "Of course reporters being what they are, they immediately called other reporters who were not in the court and who were not bound by the gag order, and they told the story."

A few months later, the imam was served with a "show cause" letter to answer for his actions. There was another hearing, and this time Hoslan had legal representation: famed lawyer and opposition leader Karpal Singh. The lawyer pleaded for leniency, arguing that his client regretted his actions and had apologized to the court. Karpal Singh also pointed out that the man had a wife and seven children between the ages of six and sixteen. The judges refused, however, and sentenced the imam to a one-year jail term for contempt in the face of the court. Before passing judgment, the head of the three-judge panel read a statement that said, in part, "any criticism of a judge or the decision of the court must be done in a proper manner with good intentions. Not with verbal abuse or such actions. . . . This is not to assuage our own personal dignity, but to protect the dignity and eminence of the court."[14] The imam went straight to prison.

Several hours after filing the story, Hazlan Zakaria sent an email to the rest of the *Malaysiakini* editorial group. Pricked by his conscience, he asked if in this case "we may have precipitated action which caused a man to lose one year of his life to a prison term."[15] Pointing out that without media reports such as those published in the alternative news portals *Malaysiakini* and *The Malaysian Insider*, the Federal Court might not have felt compelled to take action. Raising the question of whether the judges had initiated contempt proceedings "because our story on the incident had incited the public to deride the judiciary," Hazlan Zakaria wrote:

> It was posited that the court may have not taken such drastic measures and issued such heavy punishment if the matter was not made much of by us and stirred to the high heavens.
>
> I agree our judiciary has rot inside but on a case to case basis only. On the whole they have some integrity and need to be respected to function.
>
> Granted it was a story people love to read but I now wonder if it was judicious of us to allow the news to be published on our site.

Both of these cases appear to violate fundamental teachings of Islam. How could this happen? In Malaysia, where all of the mainstream media are controlled by individuals or groups who are close to Barisan Nasional, the ruling National Front coalition (Brown 2005, 39–56), "trial by the media" occurs when the state-controlled media launch systematic campaigns against individuals at the behest of their political bosses. Whether it was the campaign of the Mahathir government against the Sufi revivalist Al Arqam movement, or the two different cases of sodomy that were brought against Anwar Ibrahim, the pattern was the same: the state-controlled media endlessly repeated unproven charges.

The Anwar sex video provides a classic example of this pattern, and Wan Azizah, quoted earlier, put what she called "trial by the media" in the context of *fitnah* and egregious violation of fundamental Islamic principles. Interestingly, Hazlan Zakaria noted something similar in his criticism of his own employer, *Malaysiakini*, and of other alternative media in the case of the shoe-throwing imam: it was only after the opposition parties realized that the bad-tempered imam was a useful means of criticizing the integrity of the court that his case became a cause célèbre. In pursuing a sensational story, the alternative media had allowed itself to be used by political interests, with no attention paid to human consequences.

Although it may be obvious to all journalists that it would be impossible to conduct an investigation if nothing could be reported until it has been proven in court, for Muslim journalists the standards are slightly different—and higher. As *Malaysiakini*'s Hazlan Zakaria put it, just as the proper way for a Muslim scientist to do research "is to look into ways to improve life," a Muslim journalist must always be thinking about the good of humanity. While pursuing scientific knowledge, he said, "You are not supposed to . . . do things that are proscribed by the teachings." Similarly, journalists should not report on things for the sensational value but rather for the good of society. "We are taught that every job we do is a form of *ibadah*, a form of worship," he concluded. "That is why we begin everything we do in God's name, and try to do it the best we can."[16] The implications of Hazlan's statement are clear: for those who see journalism not as a vocation but rather as a form of worship, "trial by the press" violates not only the ethics of journalism but also God's fundamental law.

As with everything in Malaysia, the practice of journalism at *Malaysiakini* is affected by the same divisions of ethnicity and religion that plague the rest of the country; it is also more complicated than it looks. When I first met Fauwaz Abdul Aziz in 2007, he said that at *Malaysiakini* there is "an agreement that here we are going to disagree." When I asked if he felt that his views were valued at *Malaysiakini*, he said that there is a tolerance of difference, a balance. "I have a genuine respect for the people I work with," he said, "more so sometimes than I have for the people of my own faith. They give me lots of leeway to write what I want."

The concept that you don't have to be Muslim to practice Islamic values is something I have heard repeatedly from Muslim journalists at *Malaysiakini*. Hazlan Zakaria, for example, spoke at length on the relationship between *Malaysiakini* and the values of Islam, and how this contrasted with the policies and lifestyles of the heads of government and the heads of state (i.e., the sultans) who are entrusted with guarding the values of Islam:

> Well, [*Malaysiakini*] is secular in the fact that it does not espouse Islam, but it tallies with Islam in certain ways. We are a fairly democratic institution. There is a lot of consultation going on. What we try to do is [create] a flat organization; there is almost no barrier between top management and people on the ground. These are actually Islamic principles. So although it

does not espouse Islam—it is a secular organization—it practices Islamic values.

The people who truly understand what Islam stands for would say that in Malaysia the heads of government and the heads of Islam for each state are not practicing the Islamic lifestyle. Despite the fact that they are the heads of Islam, and that the government of Malaysia is supposed to be an Islamic state, you can see from their policies and the way they live that they do not espouse Islam.

The "agreement to disagree" between some Malay Muslims at *Malaysiakini* and others is not surprising, given the politicization of Islam in Malaysia. Indrani Kopal, one of *Malaysiakini*'s former video editors and now an award-winning documentarian, has noted "[there has been] the Islamization of everything, we tend to highlight it in our news. [Our] focus has always been seen as more antigovernment, but it's anti-Islamization as well. And the Malays who end up at *Malaysiakini* are liberal Malays."

Although *Malaysiakini*'s Malay journalists may indeed be liberal in terms of politics, many are not liberal in terms of religion. How do these journalists reconcile their religious values with the work that they do at *Malaysiakini*? In the same way Muslim journalists at the other publications do: by emphasizing the importance in Islam of truth, critical thinking, and reporting the facts. Abdul Hafiz Mohammad Yatim, *Malaysiakini*'s court reporter and a self-described conservative Muslim, said that religion is always in the background of his thoughts "because in Islam, you are a Muslim first." Hafiz contrasted his work at *Malaysiakini* with his more than ten years of working in Malaysia's mainstream media, which he described as characterized by considerable self-censorship. "In *Malaysiakini*," he concluded, "we can report the news. Just relay the facts, which is more what I think news should be."

Or, as Aidila Razak put it, "I feel this massive obligation to the truth." The difference between the Western notion of "freedom" and the more Islamic focus on justice and community values that we see in both Malaysia and Indonesia was nicely summed up by *Malaysiakini*'s CEO Premesh Chandran, who said:

I think that the politics of Islam, when they see the West, they see freedom as extravagant—as showing off your body, as detached from any sense of responsibility, or from any sense of the collective. And that freedom would be alien. Why would we want that kind of freedom? What would that kind of freedom do to the collective? It is seen as irrational. But when freedom is connected to principles like justice, like supporting the victims, it is very much grounded in a collective reality. Justice is a collective thing. Helping the victims is a collective thing. So when we ground freedom in that reality, it makes perfect sense.

The question, Premesh went on to ask, is "how do we find models to allow for religious debate?" This has been the challenge for *Malaysiakini* since its inception as well as for the modern nation of Malaysia.

FIVE

TEMPO

Cosmopolitan Islam in Practice

IN 1993, Indonesia's preeminent newsweekly *Tempo* reported on the founding of *Republika* newspaper with the headline "Cosmopolitan Islam in News." *Tempo* was owned and operated by a predominantly Muslim staff, but as Robert Hefner (1997b, 88) has noted, the magazine itself was "unabashedly independent and nonconfessional, consistent with the brightly cosmopolitan and pluralist tastes of its staff and elite readership." Eight years later, with President Soeharto out of office and an end to the restrictive regulations that had made it almost impossible for new publications to enter the market, the "Reform Era" brought with it a plethora of new newspapers and magazines. One of these publications was *Koran Tempo* (*Tempo* newspaper) under the leadership of chief editor Malela Mahargasarie. When Malela rushed to staff his paper in preparation for its launch in April 2001, eighteen of the new reporters and editors he hired had previously been with *Republika*. Many later said they brought the banner of "cosmopolitan Islam" with them to *Tempo*. Yet what did cosmopolitan Islam mean in practice?

COSMOPOLITANISM AND JOURNALISM

Coauthors Steven Vertovec and Robin Cohen (2002, 20) have noted that fundamentalism, "which celebrates exclusivity," is the enemy of cosmopolitanism. Since its founding in 1971, *Tempo* has stimulated cosmopolitan awareness and highlighted cosmopolitan practices—many of them focused on one of Indonesia's greatest preoccupations: the role and practice of Islam in the modern state (Assyaukanie 2009). As Goenawan Mohamad, the founding editor of *Tempo*, observed in 2009: "Indonesia is not exactly secular, and it is

Former *Tempo* editor Goenawan Mohamad, 1994. Photo courtesy of *Tempo*/Rully Kesuma.

not exactly religious either. When they talk about secular parties, or how Indonesia is a secular country, they are wrong." In an analysis of Islamic political thought in Indonesia, political scientist Jeremy Menchik (2016) has argued that the Indonesian mass organizations Nahdlatul Ulama (NU) and Muhammadiyah endorse tolerance without liberalism based on a set of values he calls "communal tolerance." Different from the model of "secular-liberal tolerance rooted in individual rights, the separation of church and state, and state neutrality toward religion," NU and Muhammadiyah "support tolerance based on group rights, legal pluralism, and the separation of religious and social affairs" (ibid., 124).

Unlike NU and Muhammadiyah, *Tempo* is, of course, a news organization. It is politically liberal but not secular. Just as Menchik has noted the importance of understanding that religious differences can be tolerated in societies that are not liberal, there are justifications for cosmopolitan ideas and practices in journalism other than those derived from the liberal, enlightenment model. *Tempo* has demonstrated "cosmopolitan Islam" in a number of ways: by serving as an independent monitor of power, by reporting on renewal in Islamic thinking, and by giving voice to the voiceless, including marginalized groups within Islam. Established in 1971, *Tempo* is Indonesia's leading weekly news magazine. Today *Tempo* is known for its hard-hitting editorial leaders and journalistic independence, but the magazine did not always enjoy such freedoms.

Under Soeharto's authoritarian New Order regime, *Tempo* journalists developed a set of strategies designed to protect the magazine. But sometimes these strategies were not enough, and in 1994 *Tempo* was banned, ostensibly because of a cover story on the purchase of thirty-nine used East German warships. Although the real reason they were forced to close remains unknown (the official document stated only that the story had "disturbed national security while failing to safeguard the Pancasila press"), most analysts agree that the magazine had embarrassed the regime by reporting on infighting (Steele 2005). With Soeharto's fall in 1998, *Tempo* returned to publication with greater journalistic zeal than ever. Today *Tempo* is known for its independence and willingness to question cherished cultural beliefs, be they religion, nationalism, or deference to authority. The magazine is a strong defender of pluralism and the rights of religious minorities; founding editor Goenawan Mohamad is well known for his sharp criticism of those fired by "religious egoism" who seem to "feel that they represent the voice of God and the voice of Islam, although it is not clear from where they received their mandate" (quoted in Steele 2006). Arif Zulkifli, the current chief editor, expressed these same pluralist values when he noted a controversy over a Ramadan banner in Aceh that stated "honor those who fast." Arif said: "So the sign says that Islamic people want to be acknowledged, want to be honored by non-Muslim people who don't fast. Why don't they make a banner that says 'honor those who don't fast?' Now *they* are the minority."

When I began my research on *Tempo* in 1997, I was not thinking about Islam. At that time I was interested in *Tempo*'s role as an independent weekly: both a product of the New Order and, after its banning, an important symbol of the pro-democracy movement that ultimately led to Soeharto's downfall. Although I included a chapter on the 1984 Tanjung Priok incident, in which dozens of working class Muslims were shot dead by the military in a confrontation that may well have been sparked by the regime, I gave only passing attention to what at the time several young intellectuals (significantly, Ulil Abshar-Abdalla) said was one of *Tempo*'s most important contributions: the role it had played in publicizing the work of Islamic scholar Nurcholish Madjid and the "renewal in Islamic thinking."

Later, when my focus changed to exploring the relationship between the principles of journalism and the values of Islam, I returned to *Tempo*, asking many of my earlier sources whether they saw a relationship between their work and the teachings of Islam. Although nearly all of them drew upon examples from the Qur'an and the Hadith in explaining certain aspects of journalism (including truth, balance, verification, and independence from political power), each was equally insistent that *Tempo* was in no way "Islamic." *Tempo* was pluralist, most of my sources said. As Arif Zulkifli, now the chief editor of *Tempo* magazine told me: "Although I'm from a family that is very Islamic, my profession as a journalist opened me, opened my eyes to the idea that truth doesn't only come from Islam." Arif's statement suggests not only a negotiation between two different identities—pious Muslim and

Tempo editor Arif Zulkifly, 2016. Photo courtesy of *Tempo*.

professional journalist—but also the kind of relativism that makes *Tempo* so dangerous in the eyes of "counter-cosmopolitans" (Appiah 2006, 137–43) like the journalists who wrote for *Sabili.*

As international communication scholar Gholam Khiabany (2006) has argued, "Islamic" media must be viewed within local political and economic contexts, and the development of journalism in postcolonial Indonesia has been marked by struggles against authoritarianism. Most of the senior journalists working in Indonesia came of age under Soeharto's New Order regime. In this restrictive atmosphere Islam provided one of the few legitimate means of challenging authoritarianism. During the New Order many individuals who became *Tempo* journalists were involved either formally or informally with Islamic student organizations. In the 1990s, Arif Zulkifli was part of the Islamic student movement at the University of Indonesia that eventually became the Prosperous Justice Party (Partai Keadilan Sejahtera, PKS). Ahmad Taufik was a Muslim student activist in Bandung and upon graduation worked for an Islamic cultural magazine called *Kiblat.* Bina Bektiati spoke for many of her colleagues when she said that at *Tempo* "most of us learned values from our friends and at the campus mosque." She explained, "It was the Soeharto era, and the mosque was seen as a place to discuss politics."

Many of the journalists who worked at *Tempo* during the Soeharto years have said that they joined the magazine because of its independence from the regime. Toriq Hadad, a former chief editor, put it in Islamic terms when he explained that when he joined *Tempo* in the 1980s, he was attracted to the magazine precisely for this reason. "In Islam," Toriq said, "an ulama [religious scholar] has the most difficult of all duties because he cannot associate with people who are close to power. An ulama is the person who must control power. And *Tempo* is a magazine that would often point out if a *kyai* [religious teacher and scholar] was playing with power." Toriq added that he knew, perhaps subconsciously, that this was the right path, "to speak for justice without siding with power. Power needs limits. Power must be reined in." He said: "And I thought this magazine [*Tempo*] was exactly right. *Tempo* had values that were in keeping with my views about life and about truth."

Mohammad Hashim Kamali (2002, 23) cited numerous examples from the Qur'an and the Hadith of the importance of speaking truth to power, including the Prophet's oft-quoted statement that "the best form of Jihad is to tell a word of truth to an oppressive ruler." Many Muslim journalists at

Tempo and elsewhere mentioned this passage—along with the sayings of the first two Caliphs that the people should correct them if they deviate from the truth (Galandar 2008). As Amarzan Loebis, a senior *Tempo* editor, said, "the Prophet is a person who sends a message. And I try to be a journalist who sends a message to other people. The message is what? To remind, and to have a critical attitude. So if there is something wrong that is done by another person, or by an institution, or by the government, we have to show it." The late Syu'bah Asa, one of *Tempo*'s most famous journalists during the 1980s, explained in 2000 that even as the editor of the Islamic magazine *Panji Masyarakat* he saw his job as defending Islamic values, not particular groups of Muslims. "For me, Islamic organizations are not as important as Islamic values," he said. Under Soeharto, Muslims had been treated unjustly. "But if Muslims treat others unjustly, we criticize them too."

Scholars have noted that in Islam "forbidding wrong" is paramount, and Muslims have an obligation to stop evil when they see it (Cook 2003). As previously noted, in the Hadith the Prophet Muhammad is quoted as saying, "Whoever sees a wrong, and is able to put it right . . . with his hand, let him do so; if he can't, then with his tongue; if he can't then in his heart, and that is the bare minimum of faith" (quoted in Cook 2003, 4.) In Indonesia the "watchdog" role of the press is grounded in the obligation of Muslims to stop evil when they see it, and for much of Indonesian press history "evil" was related to the political context of the New Order. For example, the injustice of a political system in which there were virtually no limits to the government's authority led *Tempo* magazine writers to lend subtle support to ordinary people in their struggle against the overwhelming power of the state. A content analysis of nearly twenty-five years of the national section of *Tempo* during the Soeharto era (Steele 2005) revealed a disproportionate number of stories with "victims" as the main actors.

Today, in many cases the victims are other groups of Muslims, marginalized and oppressed by the mainstream majority. In commenting on one of these groups, the Ahmadiyah, Toriq Hadad said: "I see the problem of Ahmadiyah as an issue of justice. They have been treated unjustly. *Tempo*'s coverage of Ahmadiyah has been extraordinary and very much in line with democracy. We have to see it not from the perspective of religion but rather from democracy. How can a small group not get the same rights as the others? This is a matter of justice—why can some groups use the name of Islam while Ahmadiyah cannot? It is not fair. This is the view of *Tempo*."

When I recently told *Tempo*'s founding editor Goenawan Mohamad that I was struck by the magazine's role in publicizing the ideas of Nurcholish Madjid during the 1980s, he seemed surprised. "We were always interested in ideas," he said, "so naturally when someone is talking about secularizing Islam, this is big news." Indeed, Goenawan and his friends had been interested in ideas and intellectual freedom since the 1960s, the days of their signing of the *Manifesto Kebudayaan* (Cultural manifesto), which was known derisively as *Manikebu*.[1] If one of their enemies was the intellectual rigidity of the Soekarno regime, in this they found common cause with another marginalized group: educated Muslim intellectuals who had roots in the political party Masyumi (Majelis Syuro Muslimin Indonesia, or the Indonesian Muslim Consultative Council). "You have to put *Tempo* in a continuum of ideas, the battle of ideas from the beginning of the republic," Goenawan said. "Under Soekarno, the Muslims were really persecuted. Jailed, tortured, and then when the killings—they had the grudges about the Communists. When Soekarno collapsed, the Muslims who were HMI [Himpunan Mahasiswa Islam, or the Muslim Students Association] were in the leading part of the anti-Soekarno, anti-Communist movement."

In writing about Islam, cultural hybridity, and cosmopolitanism, historian Carool Kersten (2009) has cited Nikos Papastergiadis's discussion of the "unresolved paradoxes, dualities, centrifugal, and centripetal forces underlying the synergies that produce cultural hybridity and cosmopolitanism." Noting that there is a "shadowy" side to the cultural hybridity of the new Muslim intelligentsia, Kersten quotes Papastergiadis's observation that "if the non-Western is to enter the West, it must do so in the guise of . . . the non-Western Westerner" (ibid., 93). Since its founding in 1971, Goenawan Mohamad's *Tempo* had been the magazine of the "non-Western Westerner" par excellence. Founded by writers and student activists who, like Goenawan, had been associated with the anti-Soekarno "Generation of '66," many were close to the other banned party, the Indonesian Socialist Party (Partai Sosialis Indonesia, PSI) (Steele 2005).

The PSI was widely considered to be a party of "salon socialists" or "liberals" living in the wealthy Jakarta suburb of Menteng. Closely resembling the European democratic-socialist parties that had influenced PSI founder Sutan Syahir, the PSI was notable for its "concern for individual freedom" and "openness to world intellectual currents" (Feith and Castles 1970, 227). In 1960, Soekarno banned the PSI, along with the Islamic party Masyumi, because of its role in the regional rebellions of 1958. Political scientist Harold Crouch (1988, 179n1) has asserted that many Javanese Army officers disliked the PSI, viewing them as "westernized intellectuals [with a] 'superiority complex.'" Associated with the anti-Communist "modernizers" and Berkeley-trained technocrats who wanted to bring stability and rational planning to Indonesia's economy, in its early days *Tempo* was a strong supporter of the economic policies of Soeharto's New Order government. Part of the "modernization project" of the 1960s, the technocrats were influenced by Western development theorists who espoused programs designed to show the superiority of American liberalism over Marxism. Soeharto's New Order government, with its vigorous opposition to Communism and its weakened economy, was especially ripe for developmentalism.

MUKTI ALI AND SOEHARTO'S POLICY TOWARD ISLAM

Paralleling Soeharto's desire to keep the extreme left of Communism at bay was his desire to control what his administration saw as the extreme right of Islam. The Cabinet minister tasked with this job in the Ministry of Religious Affairs was Mukti Ali. A member of Masyumi, Mukti Ali had roots in the *pesantren* (boarding school) culture of East Java, Arabic literature and Islamic history at the University of Karachi, and the scholarship of "Western-orientalist scholars who wrote on Islam" whom he had met when he studied comparative religion at McGill University in Canada (Munhanif 1996, 90). At McGill he developed a close friendship with comparative religion scholar Wilfred Cantwel Smith and came to see Islamic studies in what he later described as a "holistic" fashion (ibid., 92). According to Mukti Ali's biographer:

> At McGill, too, he [Mukti Ali] found the primary aim of studying Islam, or religion, to be a total attempt of how a religious tradition can adapt itself to the challenges of modernization. To this end, he assert[ed] the need for introducing an empirical approach to Islam as a means of re-interpretation of its doctrines in the context of modernity. For Mukti Ali, such an approach to Islam, which is often ignored by Islamic traditional instructions in pesantren, would bring Islam and the Muslim society to accept and even sympathize with some important discourses of modernism such as

intellectual freedom, the concept of the state, the rights of women, and dialogue among religious communities. (Ibid., 92–93)

Upon returning to Indonesia, Mukti Ali found a job with the Ministry of Religious Affairs. In 1960 he was appointed to lead departments of comparative religion at the state institutes for Islamic studies in both Jakarta and Yogyakarta, and to formulate a curriculum for the new program of study.

As political scientist Ali Munhanif (ibid., 96) has noted, many Indonesian Muslims were suspicious of the science of comparative religion, assuming that it was imported from the West and thus "an intellectual stigma or crime." Mukti Ali sharply disagreed. In his view, not only was it medieval Muslim scholars who had "established the foundation of the methodology of comparative religions," but the spirit of respect and appreciation for other world religions was vital in Indonesia, if religious pluralism was to be preserved. His 1965 book, *Ilmu Perbandingan Agama: Pengantar tentang Metode dan Sistema* (The science of comparative religions: Introduction to methods and systems) became the standard text at the state institutes of Islamic studies, or IAIN (Institut Agama Islam Negeri) (ibid., 125n25).

In answer to the question of whether the study of comparative religion was dangerous for a good Muslim, Mukti Ali argued that "comparative religion should be intended to understand how God has revealed his religion to mankind through His prophets, and how mankind tries to respond to it." Although it was "understandable" that the scholar might want to make a judgment as to whether the characteristics of a certain religious community were "true or false," this was not his task (ibid., 99). Mukti Ali saw the study of comparative religion not as an academic exercise but rather as a call to be concerned with interreligious dialogue. This would become a hallmark not only of his own work but also of the IAIN, and indeed the Ministry of Religious Affairs under Soeharto.

In 1964, Mukti Ali was appointed as the rector's assistant for public affairs at the IAIN in Yogyakarta. One of his most notable accomplishments was the influence he had over a group of young students and intellectuals who were residing there in the late 1960s, a circle that became known as the "Limited Group." Hosting a series of meetings in his home, Mukti Ali's study circle has been described as "a stepping stone of the 'Renewal Movement of Islamic Thought'" in Indonesia. The group included Djohan Effendi,

Dawam Rahardjo, and future *Tempo* writers Ahmad Wahib and Syu'bah Asa (ibid., 100).[2] Goenawan Mohamad explained it was Syu'bah Asa who brought Ahmad Wahib to *Tempo*. Although Ahmad Wahib became famous for the luminous diary that was published after his 1973 death in a motorcycle accident, at the time he was hired none of his *Tempo* colleagues considered him to be an especially important thinker. Goenawan recalled that when *Tempo* decided to do a cover story on the renewal in Islamic thinking, Syu'bah assigned Wahib to interview Nurcholish Madjid "because he knew him." They had belonged to the same group in Yogyakarta.

Goenawan laughed, then explained that during the interview, "Nurcholish said to Wahib, 'Why do you ask me? You know about this.'"

"And Wahib said, 'I am a reporter now.'"

NURCHOLISH MADJID AND THE RENEWAL IN ISLAMIC THINKING

"For me political Islam is wrong," Goenawan Mohamad said. "Personally wrong. I don't believe in the Islamic state. And Nurcholish did amazing things. Nurcholish was the one to say it, and the right person to say it. If I were to say it, I would be an easy target." During the 1970s and 1980s, *Tempo* became known for a series of articles that highlighted the thinking of those who argued that what was really needed in Indonesia was a renewal in Islamic thought. Goenawan Mohamad himself noted that "*Tempo* was the first to introduce Nurcholish Madjid's ideas. And Gus Dur [Abdurrahman Wahid] was a columnist. So the language of the so-called liberal Islam was there from the beginning."

Nurcholish Madjid was a brilliant thinker and writer who earned his PhD at the University of Chicago under the supervision of Fazlur Rahman, a noted neomodernist scholar (Kersten 2009, 115). Although the phrase "renewal in Islam" is usually associated with Nurcholish Madjid, anthropologist Robert Hefner (2000, 113) has pointed out that Nurcholish was a shining star among a constellation of other like-minded intellectuals, which included Mukti Ali's "Limited Group."

In the early 1970s this group of young modernist Muslim scholars developed a new strategy for social change. Suspicious of mass politics, they argued that Indonesian Muslims had been sidetracked by the debate over the creation of an Islamic state. Not only was this impractical given the realities of the New Order, but it was also not in keeping with the teachings of the

Qur'an, which they argued never mandated an Islamic state. What was important, they said, was that Muslims preserve what is sacred in Islam, while distinguishing the divine from what is merely human. Nurcholish concluded that Islam needed to "secularize" (or rather "desacralize") Muslim political parties. "Islam itself, if examined truthfully," Nurcholish wrote, "was begun with a process of secularization. Indeed, the principle of *tawhid* [the uncompromised oneness of God] represents the starting point for a much larger secularization" (quoted in Hefner 2000, 117). As Nurcholish defined it, "secularization is the ability to distinguish between transcendental and temporal values. This secularization is also intended to develop an understanding that humans are God's vice-regents in this world; they are given the freedom to choose and decide for themselves and at the same time have to bear responsibility for their actions before God" (quoted in An-Na'im 2008, 265).

After the Soeharto regime passed laws requiring Pancasila to become the sole basis of all social and political organizations in the mid-1980s, renewal in Islamic thought became even more politically salient. *Tempo* did a number of cover stories on the challenges facing Islam, most of which were written by Syu'bah Asa. As political scientist William Liddle (1996b, 271) noted, the scripturalist Islamic publication *Media Dakwah* saw *Tempo* as one of the "enemies of Islam, largely because of its promotion of Nurcholish Madjid, whom *Media Dakwah* view[ed] as an 'apostate.'" An example of the kind of story of which scripturalist Muslims disapproved ran in *Tempo* in December 1984. Titled "Does Islam Include a Concept of Statehood?," the story summarized a series of interviews with prominent Muslim scholars, including both Nurcholish Madjid and Abdurrahman Wahid, and concluded:

> Based on the statements of those who were interviewed by *Tempo*, it can be
> affirmed that in neither the Quran nor the Hadis—or even more generally
> in the laws pertaining to ritual obligations—is there a command for an
> Islamic state. At least not in the sense of requiring a particular shape or
> model. "The problem with Iran," said Abdurrahman Wahid, for example,
> "is that because they believe their state is the one and only model of Islam,
> they then attack the form of the state of Saudi Arabia, etc."
>
> Generally speaking, it can be agreed that Islam contains regulations for
> society, and not for the state itself. Certainly the ideal Islamic society will
> reflect the teachings of Islam, and at maximum, Islamic law. And indeed
> Islamic law requires the protection of the state, in whatever form that

protection might take. But what is going on here right now is actually an even more fundamental discussion: the issue is how far Islamic law can change.

Significantly, Syu'bah Asa, who wrote the stories, gave Goenawan Mohamad full credit for this series of articles. "Okay, in a technical sense, I may have known more about the issues compared with Goenawan," Syu'bah said. But on topics like secularization, "Islamic vision," and the conviction that the thoughts of Nurcholish had to be included in *Tempo*, "we were the same." Although Syu'bah wrote the articles, he said that Goenawan Mohamad was the "visionary."

"Goenawan said we must defend the Islamic community because they have been treated unjustly," Syu'bah explained. "And if it turns out that Islam treats others unfairly, then we'll strike at Islam." Syu'bah concluded that *Tempo* was safe because the magazine treated each branch of Islamic thought fairly. "We defended them all," he said. "It was Goenawan's design. I only implemented it." In their rejection of the Islamic state, their support for *ijtihad* (independent theological reasoning), their contextual interpretation of Islamic texts, and their support for the concept of modernization, the thinking of the neomodernists was thus very much in keeping not only with the developmentalism of the New Order but also with the aims of the founders of *Tempo* magazine, which gave voice to their aspirations and thinking.

THE FOUNDING OF *KORAN TEMPO*

In 2001 the Tempo Media Group launched a daily newspaper called *Koran Tempo*. Like its magazine namesake, *Tempo* newspaper prides itself on being a defender of the rights of religious minorities—even the Islamic religious movement Ahmadiyah, which the Indonesian government has labeled "deviant." Significantly, eighteen of the new reporters hired by founding chief editor Malela Mahargasarie were from *Republika*. Malela explains that he hired the large group from *Republika* because he knew they had been trained by ex-*Tempo* journalists Farid Gaban and Zaim Uchrowi, and because he knew that as newspaper journalists they would have a different approach to covering the news than did his colleagues at the magazine. "There were two things," he said. "First, I saw them as journalists that couldn't be bribed, and second, I wanted journalists who would be appropriate for a newspaper."

Although Malela is uncomfortable with the term "Islamic"—and most Indonesians would not view *Tempo* as such—approximately 80 percent of the news organization's editorial staff is Muslim. As Malela said, "We do not wave the flag of Islam." Yet some of the ex-*Republika* journalists are more willing to address the relationship between *Tempo* and cosmopolitan Islam. *Tempo* journalist Burhan Sholihin said:

> The Islamic values that are more universal, like fighting corruption, etc. were taken [to *Tempo*] by those who left *Republika*. There were many different reasons why people left. Some, for example, didn't like the political conflict inside. And when *Tempo* newspaper was founded, its goals were the same mix. When Malela wanted to create a newspaper, his goals were the same: to make a newspaper that was progressive to improve the nation. At the beginning, Malela was more inclined to say, okay, the market is Islam, but the name isn't Islam. He wanted the name of Islam to be in the background, not to be labeled Islam. But the struggle is the same.

Most of the *Tempo* journalists with whom I have spoken are clear not only about substantial Islam but also about founding editor Goenawan Mohamad's role in promoting this way of thinking. Zaim Uchrowi, for example, a former *Tempo* journalist and one of the founding editors of the newspaper *Berita Buana* that was later absorbed into *Republika*, explained: "I don't believe too much in Islamic symbols. I believe in Islamic values. So when we talk about the Islamic press, for us, the press is the press. Media is media. Not Islamic media and non-Islamic media, no. Media is media. When I joined *Tempo* [in 1983] my views were very much in keeping with what Goenawan Mohamad wrote in the very first issue of *Tempo* in 1971 when it was founded: that truth and un-truth are not monopolized by any one side.[3] Therefore the method of thinking at *Tempo* was very strong: We didn't defend a group, we defended truth." To Zaim, the idea that there was no such thing as "100 percent truth" was directly related to the thinking of Nurcholish Madjid. He explained:

> Nurcholish Madjid said in the early 1970s that the problem with Muslims in Indonesia is that they cannot differentiate between *Tuhan* [God] with a big T and a little t. Meaning that in Indonesia, everything is sacralized. And

this means that we don't have relativity towards truth, and this becomes the problem. According to Nurcholish, the only thing that should be sacralized is God. Religion teaches that truth is actually relative, except for the Truth that's one. This for me is the connection between the world of journalism that I got from Goenawan, the point of view of Nurcholish, and the teachings of religion that I received when I was young from my family. . . . So for me, yes, in journalism *Tempo* is Islamic, and, from my perspective, *Sabili* and *Republika* are actually less Islamic, because they are colonized by their own symbols.

This intellectual skepticism, along with the idea of defending the truth rather than a particular group, distinguishes *Tempo* from Indonesian media that calls itself "Islamic" and is also an important aspect of what makes the publication "cosmopolitan." Yet for the journalists who work at *Tempo* and who think about such matters, these ideas are also very much in keeping with the teachings of Islam—which, according to *Tempo* editor Yos Rizal, is to be *raḥmatan li al-ʿalamin* ("a blessing to all mankind"):

The content of *Tempo* newspaper isn't labeled Islamic. No label. But I think there is the enthusiasm for Islamic values in the understanding of universal values. In lots of matters—if there isn't justice, or tolerance, or if there's the oppression of those who are in a minority, these are the challenges. In fact, the principle of the Qur'an is that 'to you your religion, to me my religion'— the principle of difference has to be valued. This is what should emerge in a publication that is labeled Islamic. For example, in *Republika* it often comes out that the Ahmadiyah people should repent, things like that. But in our paper there is a sense among the editors that your religion is a personal matter between you and God. We have to value that.

TEMPO AND THE JARINGAN ISLAM LIBERAL

For the enemies of *Tempo*, nothing grates more than its purported support of the Jaringan Islam Liberal (JIL, or Liberal Islamic Network). A quick Google search of "*Tempo*" and "Jaringan Islam Liberal" comes up with tens of thousands of links, many of them to websites and blog postings that are remarkably vicious in their criticisms of both. JIL was founded at the Utan Kayu Community, and one history of JIL gives Goenawan Mohamad credit for having overseen its creation (Ali 2005, 4). It began with a meeting in

January 2001, at which Ulil Abshar-Abdalla, Luthfi Assyaukani, Hamid Basyaib, Ihsan Ali Fauzi, Nong Darol Mahmada, and Ahmad Sahal discussed with Goenawan the possibility of establishing a network of intellectuals and activists concerned with liberal interpretations of Islamic teachings that might serve to counter fundamentalist discourse. Ulil was quoted as saying, "We've seen radical Islam grow militant, systematic, and organized, while 'liberal Islam' has been unorganized, weak, not militant, not resistant, and unassertive in giving voice to its perspective" (ibid., 4).

The wave of violence and rise of fundamentalism that emerged after the fall of Soeharto may have been the trigger for the establishment of JIL, but it had clear antecedents in the movement for renewal in Islam of the 1970s and 1980s (Nurdin 2005, 24). Most of the young intellectuals who established JIL grew up in the culture of Nahdhatul Ulama (NU) and were not only steeped in the intellectual tradition of Gus Dur but also well versed in the thinking of Nurcholish Madjid and the other neomodernists associated with the earlier movement. Like the previous generation of reformers, they drew upon the early twentieth-century modernist tradition established by Muhammad 'Abduh. In this regard they were self-consciously part of the centuries-long cosmopolitan tradition linking Indonesia with the Middle East that has been noted by scholars in a variety of fields (Azra 1992; Tagliacozzo 2009).

Though indebted to many reform traditions in both the Malay Archipelago and elsewhere, the young intellectuals of JIL took their name from the 1998 work of sociologist Charles Kurzman, *Liberal Islam: A Sourcebook* (Ali 2005, 5). Almost immediately the problem with the name became evident: it was too closely associated with the economic neoliberalism promoted by the International Monetary Fund (IMF), the World Bank, and the development-oriented economists of the New Order itself. It is this use of Western sources in defending their ideas that has made JIL especially open to attacks from conservatives and "susceptible to identification with a Western agenda" (Nurdin 2005, 34). From the beginning, there was a debate over the meaning of the term *liberal*, although it eventually came to be seen as "the spirit of freedom of thought and expression" (Ali 2005, 9). As the group maintained that JIL was a network, not an organization or party, there was no binding agreement as to terms, but eventually they came to agree that liberal Islam meant "a liberal and liberating form of Islam that emphasizes ethics rather than formalism, stresses relativism and inclusivism rather than absolutism, promotes the interests of the minority and of the oppressed, and supports religious freedom and the separation of religion and politics" (ibid., 9–10).

In almost every regard, these are the same views held by journalists at *Tempo*. JIL has been especially adept at using the mass media. Their website (www.islamlib.com), although no longer well maintained, was for many years a sourcebook for information about the network. Utilizing their space at the Utan Kayu Community, they had regular talk shows on Radio 68H, which were broadcast to a network of more than fifty stations in Indonesia. In addition to holding numerous programs and discussions, they also maintained a book-publishing program. One of their most innovative moves was to set up a syndicated page with the *Jawa Pos*, East Java's biggest newspaper—the owners of which overlap with the owners of *Tempo*. Dahlan Iskan, a former *Tempo* journalist and the CEO of the *Jawa Pos* group, met with Goenawan Mohamad, and the two agreed that JIL would provide the newspaper with a weekly page devoted to the network. The *Jawa Pos* publishes more than forty community papers, and the syndicated material appeared in each of these as well. Dhimam Abror, who was the paper's chief editor at the time, said that the *Jawa Pos* was happy to get the content, which he edited only lightly. What he was most concerned about were the headlines, which he often changed to make sure that they weren't too "provocative." But he said that for the most part the JIL material was very well received in East Java and elsewhere.

Despite this positive reception, JIL has been demonized. *Sabili* magazine, for example, saw JIL as one of its "chief enemies" (Rijal 2005, 429) and an organization funded by foreign powers in an attempt to weaken Islam and subjugate Muslims. This view was shared by the Forum of Indonesian Islamic Scholars (Forum Umat Ulama Islam, FUUI), which in 2002 issued a fatwa stating that it was halal to shed the blood of anyone who dishonors Allah, the Prophet Muhammad, Islam, and the Islamic community—a fatwa that was widely interpreted to be a call for the death of JIL coordinator Ulil Abshar-Abdalla (Ichwan 2013, 81). The provocation was an article that Ulil had published in *Kompas* newspaper called "Rethinking Islam" (Abshar-Abdallah 2002). Less incendiary but equally poisonous was the 2005 fatwa against secularism, pluralism, and liberalism by the quasi-governmental organization Majelis Ulama Indonesia (MUI, the Indonesian Council of Muslim Scholars). Although the fatwa—which gleefully abbreviated secularism, pluralism, and liberalism into the acronym *sepilis*—was roundly denounced by a host of prominent liberal or progressive Muslim scholars, it had an immediate impact, especially on popular discourse on religious pluralism and interreligious relations (Ichwan 2013, 83).[4] *Sabili* has made eradication of the *virus sepilus* one of its major goals.

There is logic to *Sabili*'s critique of JIL, which it connects directly with Goenawan Mohamad and *Tempo* (Satria 2009). Since its founding in 1971, *Tempo* has supported modernization, a secular state, pluralism in religion, and an economic policy of development. It has also supported the rights of minorities and given voice to the aspirations of those who called for a renewal in Islamic thinking. Institut Studi Arus Informasi (ISAI, the Institute for the Study of the Free Flow of Information), founded by Goenawan Mohamad after *Tempo*'s banning, and Radio 68H (also housed at Utan Kayu) have been consistent voices for human rights and intellectual freedom. The Utan Kayu Community has received funding from Western NGOs, including the Asia Foundation, which, according to Ulil, funded the Liberal Islamic Network under an Islam and Civil Society grant. For those who are looking for conspiracies designed to weaken political Islam, there indeed seems to be one, and *Sabili* has been relentless in its attacks on *Tempo*, the Utan Kayu Community (along with its successor, Salihara), and Goenawan himself—thus lending support to the argument that the enemy of cosmopolitanism is exclusivity and narrow parochialism. As Ulil said, *Tempo* has always given "a big space" to JIL. This was natural, he said, "because JIL had a space at Utan Kayu, and Utan Kayu was established by *Tempo* friends, and *Tempo* friends felt that JIL was the new generation after Gus Dur. It was an extension," he said.

Yet despite the fact that, as Goenawan has noted, "the language of the so-called liberal Islam" had been in *Tempo* since the beginning, most *Tempo* journalists distance themselves from the liberal network. Why? To some extent, the fundamentalist campaign to demonize "liberalism" has been successful. By associating JIL with "something terrible," publications like *Sabili* have made those with liberal views afraid to be a part of it. When I commented to Goenawan in 2013 that *Tempo* people are usually dismissive of JIL, he said: "That is the result of this attack. People have started to distance themselves; this is very common in a propaganda war. But actually they share the same views. And you don't want to take sides, especially when you are a journalist. So you have to distance yourself. But I think it's the same spirit."

It is possible that Goenawan is right, yet it is also possible that *Tempo* journalists provide another example of what Menchik (2016) has called "tolerance without liberalism." Menchik's argument would explain the views of those—like many at *Tempo*—who argue that JIL is simply too provocative, engaging in battles for issues like the rights of gays and lesbians that are far removed from what should be its true mission. This is the view of former *Jawa Pos* editor Dhimam Abror, who emphasizes that it is ephemeral things—like support of gay marriage—that make people annoyed with JIL. "If it's pluralism, then yes, I am a liberal Muslim. If it's tolerance, then yes, I am a liberal Muslim. If it's secularization in the sense of Nurcholish Madjid, then yes, I am a liberal Muslim. But if it's gay marriage, interfaith marriage, or acceptance of gays and lesbians, then no, I am not liberal," he said.

Senior *Tempo* editor Idrus Shahab added another dimension to the problem with JIL—what he described as a kind of intellectual arrogance and unwillingness to engage with its conservative critics. Explaining that whereas he himself had associated with "left-leaning" Muslims while at university—like watermelons, he said, "*Islam semangka*" were red on the inside, green on the outside—liberal Islam was different: "Although each person has his own motivation, JIL is inclined to be a sort of antithesis to what is old. People in the hard-line community, they feel threatened. So their reaction to JIL is too harsh. However, in the language of Islam, if they [JIL] are *mujaddid*, renewing, reforming, they have to have hearts that aren't too high. They have to use the language of their audiences. And JIL doesn't use that language. This isn't their goal. They want to create a network of people outside of the hardliners. They don't communicate with the hardliners."

Indonesia specialist Giora Eliraz (2008, 383) has argued that the emergence of liberal Islamic thought in Indonesia is tightly connected to the transmission of themes and ideas from abroad, "continuously fed through a dialogue with liberal Islamic thinkers worldwide." Marked by an openness to engage with Western culture, the young intellectuals of JIL share with *Tempo* journalists an appreciation of what can be learned from "the other." Ulil Abshar-Abdalla's comment about his time spent in the United States echoes the early nineteenth-century work of imam al-Tahtawi, who was sent by the Ottoman viceroy of Egypt to study in Paris: "The conclusion is that we can learn many positive things from others; whoever they are" (quoted in ibid., 394).

Yet, as Toriq Hadad asked rhetorically, "Why do you have to become 'Islam liberal' in order to honor other religions?" He continued: "Growing up, in East Java, a place that's pretty orthodox, I already knew the differences. What I think has fallen off in Indonesia is the understanding of Islam in a complete manner. Therefore, sectors emerge that want to express themselves as being more Islamic than the others. For me, if we go back to the original teachings, Islam isn't something that has to be feared. For me, differences aren't something that's new. It's not a problem if I'm different from anybody."

Tempo and the institutions that it has spawned, either directly or indirectly, have in common both an attitude of openness toward others and the competence required to engage with them directly. Steeped in the notion that truth never resides in just one place, *Tempo* journalists self-consciously hold to multiple and sometimes conflicting identities. Neither secular nor necessarily even liberal, journalists at *Tempo* take a flexible stance, marked by skepticism, transparency, and a reliance on observable data. As Idrus Shahab said, "Journalism is a road toward *jihad* to reach justice, but we have to be skeptical toward everything including ourselves—and even toward journalism itself." This skepticism, along with a focus on what we share collectively as human beings, is the mark of cosmopolitanism in practice.

CONCLUSION

The Journalisms of Islam

ON THE evening of September 12, 1984, in the gritty industrial port community of Tanjung Priok on the north side of Jakarta, the Indonesian military opened fire on a group of unarmed Muslim protestors. The protestors had rallied in support of four men who had been arrested for an incident that had begun two days earlier, when a noncommissioned officer had allegedly refused to take off his shoes before entering a *mushalla* (prayer house) and used water from a nearby gutter to remove posters from the walls. The posters had urged Muslim women to wear headscarves (*jilbab*) and were considered a dangerous provocation.

According to the official version of the incident, nine Muslim rioters were shot dead by Indonesian soldiers and fifty-three more were wounded. Several Chinese-owned shops were burned by rioters, and eight bodies were found in the rubble. *Tempo* magazine's four-page account, published a few days later, challenged the government's version and raised the death toll to twenty-eight.[1] *Tempo*'s story was considered so daring that many people thought the magazine would be banned.

For twenty-seven-year old *Tempo* reporter Bambang Harymurti, who arrived in Tanjung Priok early the next morning and was one of the first journalists on the scene, the most memorable image was the blood. "When I came there," he said in 2000, "the fire brigade was still washing down the street, because there was blood. They were washing down the street." Journalists from daily papers *Kompas* and *Sinar Harapan* were also there, Bambang recalled, "but they were so sure that they were not going to be allowed to print this story anyway that they didn't write the report. But at *Tempo*, we are always operating that a reporter should report. Just report. And then the editor will decide whether it can be printed. So we have to do this job."

For Bambang and Agus Basri, the two reporters assigned to the story, doing the job entailed the usual admonition to check and recheck. But it was very difficult to find eyewitnesses. Thus they had to "follow the chain" of sources in what was still a very dangerous and unstable situation. "[Eyewitnesses] would say, 'I was there, but it happened earlier and my friend was there,' and so you go to that friend," Bambang said: "They would say, 'A thousand people were shot dead—my brother saw the bodies.' And then I went to the brother and asked, 'Were you really there?' And he would say, 'No, actually I was not there, I heard this from my neighbor.' So you keep following the line. We thought the best thing to do was a sort of chronological order of what really happened."

In their book *The Elements of Journalism*, veteran American journalists Bill Kovach and Tom Rosenstiel (2001, 79) noted that "the essence of journalism is a discipline of verification." The need to "check and recheck" is the number-one lesson for young journalists throughout the world, and Muslim journalists are no exception. Not only in the five news organizations I have studied but in every newsroom I have visited in Indonesia and Malaysia, the Qur'anic instruction that believers must be skeptical of those who come bearing news is the one most frequently cited. For example, former *Jawa Pos* editor Dhimam Abror said that the Qur'an is quite explicit on the idea of good journalism, making it clear that "if one of the faithful is approached by an unreliable person, it is his obligation to look for an explanation." Herry Nurdi, the former editor of *Sabili*, said the same thing: "In Islam it's like this, when there is a report, it is ordered in the Qur'an to verify. I have said to our friends, as Muslims, you are going to be responsible to God later, if you don't do the process of verification."

Indonesian and Malaysian journalists often mention verification within one additional context: *isnad*, or the process of following "the chain of transmission" of the sayings and acts of the Prophet and his Companions. As previously noted, *isnad* takes the form of "it has been related to me by A on the authority of B on the authority of C on the authority of D (usually a Companion of the Prophet) that Muhammad said . . . ."[2] As Iranian-American author Reza Aslan (2006, 163) has explained: "Those *hadith* whose *isnad* could be traced to an early and reliable source were considered 'sound' and accepted as authentic, while those that could not were considered 'weak' and rejected." Indonesian state Islamic university lecturer Faris Khairul Anam (2009, 57) has explicitly connected *isnad* with the process of journalistic verification in *Fikih Jurnalistik* (Journalistic jurisprudence), noting that when a journalist hears a story, he or she must ask, "Who said that? From where did you hear about this?"

Although Dhimam Abror was the first to explain to me how *isnad* was related to journalism, I had previously heard the *process* described in almost identical language ten years earlier, when *Tempo*'s Bambang Harymurti related how he had "followed the chain" of evidence in reporting on the 1984 incident at Tanjung Priok (Steele 2005). Bambang's words directly parallel the process of *isnad*. Consciously or not, he used the idiom of Islam to explain his work as a journalist, and this was how I knew I was on to something. Yet until I visited a series of Islamic universities and institutes in Indonesia and Malaysia, I still wasn't certain.

JOURNALISM TRAINING AND ISLAM

There are eighteen state Islamic universities and institutes in Indonesia, and each of them offers some sort of journalism education. Malaysia does not have a parallel network of state-run Islamic institutes, but the International Islamic University of Malaysia (IIUM) offers a program in communication in the faculty of Revealed Knowledge and Human Sciences. The basic curricula resemble those of journalism programs in the United States, with a combination of courses in theory and practice. Yet unlike the United States and other Western countries, in many Indonesian state Islamic institutes and universities, courses in journalism are located not in the social sciences or independent colleges but rather in faculties or schools of *dakwah*, where they are seen as key elements of Islamic propagation. It seemed to me that if there was indeed a strong connection between the principles of journalism and the teachings of Islam, it ought to be evident in the way these faculties trained their students.

In Indonesia, university-level training for journalists is still relatively rare, and most learn on the job (Hanitzsch 2005, 497). Many editors-in-chief express reluctance to hire graduates of university journalism or communication programs because they find that "these students [are] not well-prepared for the real challenges of the profession" (ibid., 498) or "only know about the skill of communication" (Hume 2007, 14). My own experience in teaching journalism in Indonesia supports these conclusions: be it in public, private, general, or Islamic institutes of higher education, journalism training in Indonesia tends to focus on theory rather than practical skills. Yet even this familiar scholar-versus-practitioner way of thinking about journalism training (Deuze 2006) ignores something fundamental about journalism education in Indonesia: the context of Islam.

In August 2011, which coincided with the fasting month of Ramadan, I did fieldwork at three Indonesian state Islamic institutes and universities: the Islamic State University (Universitas Islam Negara, UIN) Syarif Hidayatullah in Jakarta, UIN Sunan Kalijaga in Yogyakarta, and the State Institute of Islamic Studies (Institut Agama Islam Negeri, IAIN) Sunan Ampel in Surabaya. In October 2012, I visited a fourth, UIN Sunan Gunung Djati in Bandung, and a few months later I met with the former director of the communication program at the International Islamic University of Malaysia in Kuala Lumpur, along with one of the junior faculty members whom he had recruited.[3] At each of these universities or institutes I asked about how journalism is taught within the context of *dakwah*. The results of these meetings and interviews suggested a way of understanding journalism that is entirely different from that commonly found in the United States. For the lecturers in the *dakwah* faculties, journalism is seen as one of many means of spreading Islam and of communicating truth to the people. As Yunan Yusuf, a well-known professor of *dakwah* at UIN Jakarta, explained: "Islam is the difference, not only in symbols but also in context. When you add Islam to secular studies, they are accompanied by this difference, so when a person graduates and becomes a journalist, he will take an Islamic approach."

JOURNALISM AND *DAKWAH*

Dakwah is the Indonesian term for the Islamic concept of the call or invitation to follow the path of Allah (Ilaihi and Hefni 2007). A common way of translating *dakwah* is missionary work, or propagation of the faith. Like political scientist Harold Lasswell's famous model of communication, *dakwah* has five components: the *da'i*, or the person engaged in *dakwah*; the *mad'u*, or target audience; the channel of communication; the message; and the effect (Ilaihi 2010). A Muslim preacher giving the Friday sermon in a mosque is engaged in *dakwah*; so is a televangelist. *Dakwah* can occur in a discussion or in a conversation between two friends. It can be verbal, but it can also occur by example, in the everyday activities of a Muslim who seeks to inspire others.

Dakwah is a fundamental activity of Indonesian state Islamic institutes and universities, all of which fall under the direction of the Ministry of Religion. *Dakwah* is not only a concept, it is also the name of one of several faculties or schools. In these universities the study of communication (*ilmu komunikasi*) takes place within the *dakwah* faculty, and journalism courses are taught under the umbrella of *dakwah*. To Indonesian practitioners of *dakwah*, the connection with journalism seems obvious and is, for the most part, unquestioned. As Arief Subhan, the dean of the Dakwah and Communication Studies Faculty at UIN Jakarta explained: "Communication is something close to *dakwah*; the meaning of *dakwah* is to give a message. If you see our curriculum, you will see that nearly 75 percent is connected with communication. In addition, there are Islamic values added in, so if what is studied by our students here is compared with the University of Indonesia, it is communication plus."

Amar ma'ruf nahi munkar is a key principle of both Islam and Islamic journalism, obliging Muslims to invite good and "forbid, whether in words, acts, or silent denunciation, any evil which they see being committed" (Kamali 1998, 28). It is a phrase that came up over and over again in my discussions with lecturers at the Islamic universities and institutes as well as with their students and alumni. If the obligation to point out what is wrong is familiar to Western journalists, especially in watchdog journalism, the equal and opposite drive to invite good may be less so. H. M. Kolili, a lecturer of journalism at UIN Sunan Kalijaga Yogyakarta, explained the obligation of Muslim journalists to "motivate" their readers and to lead by providing examples of "those who are good": "When we report on the Muslim people, we have to look not only for examples of those who are bad, but also of those who are good, who have become successful, so they can become examples. With good examples, others will also want to become good. Journalistic principles and duties cannot be separated from the values of the journalists themselves, because the journalists are going to influence, to motivate." Kolili concluded: "*Amar ma'ruf* [inviting good] should be put in front of *nahi munkar* [forbidding evil]. Right now there's a lot of *nahi munkar. Amar ma'ruf* there isn't."

Although US critics often point to a lack of positive news in the news media (Weaver 1994), what Kolili describes is something different. The idea that news stories should be motivational and propel people to "do what's good" is an indication of an entirely different understanding of the purpose of journalism. Just how unique is the situation in Indonesia, where journalism is seen as being related to *dakwah* or the propagation of the faith? Several of the journalists I interviewed mentioned the goal of *jurnalisme kenabian,* which translates as "journalism of the Prophet." Azmuddin bin Ibrahim, formerly of the communication program at the International Islamic University of Malaysia, also spoke about "prophetic journalism," which he described as journalism that "follows the Prophet's teachings" and "fulfills you as a human being, not just your organization's expectations."

The American researcher Doug Underwood (2002) has described what he calls "prophetic journalism," or US reporting that draws upon the Hebrew prophetic tradition of protesting injustice and rooting out corruption. Apparent in the classic adage by nineteenth-century US journalist Finley Peter Dunne that a journalist is someone who "comforts the afflicted [and] afflicts the comfortable," the "journalism of outrage" is especially obvious in the investigative reporting of the Progressive Era. Yet, as Underwood found, many contemporary American journalists who are quick to describe themselves as secular will endorse religious values when they are couched in the language of journalism—such as the Dunne quotation—rather than in the language of the Bible.

There are indeed some similarities between the *jurnalisme kenabian* of Indonesia and prophetic journalism in the United States, but there are key differences as well. In both there is an emphasis on justice and on the corrupting influence of materialism. However, in the American use of the term, *prophetic* is taken to mean jeremiad or the telling of "hard truths about the condition of . . . society" as well as the warning of dire consequences to those who do not take heed (Underwood 2002, 22). In Indonesia, *jurnalisme kenabian* is understood more in aspirational terms or as being the kind of journalist who is "like" the Prophet Mohammad. As *Republika* editor Priyantono Oemar said, "We try to develop prophetic journalism, journalism of the Prophet. The Prophet Mohammad himself had several qualities that can be adopted and practiced in journalism. You want to give something that is true and honest, and give it in an intelligent manner. This is also what we can implement."

"WE ARE ALL *DA'I* HERE"

Although the number of graduates of Indonesian state Islamic institutes and universities who find jobs in mainstream journalism is relatively small, these numbers are deceptive. The *dakwah* faculties make explicit something that many Muslim journalists in Indonesia take for granted—that the values of journalism and the teachings of Islam are one and the same. In the words of Arys Hilman, the deputy chief editor of *Republika*: "This is where Islam is universal: justice, truth, these are teachings of Islam. We as journalists have to explain, if you are Islamic, you have to be anticorruption, you also have to be clean. If the government practices corruption, it has to be wiped out. This is also a teaching of Islam."

As Subagio Budi Parjitno, a lecturer in the department of communication studies at UIN Bandung said, "We are all *da'i* here." By explaining that "we are all engaged in *dakwah*," Budi meant that for Muslims everything one says and does is a means of sharing the message of Islam. Thus the lessons taught by the *dakwah* faculties at Indonesia's Islamic universities and institutes are relevant not only for the aspiring journalists who study there but for all Muslims. Muslim journalists at each of the publications I have analyzed have said that one should always be mindful of sharing the truth and inviting good and forbidding evil, regardless of whether one works for "Islamic" media. *Republika*'s managing editor, Elba Damhuri, said: "We as Muslim people don't always understand media. I believe that all media can be Islamic if they guard the code of ethics of journalism. Because Islam is something that isn't only in the sky, it is in our life. If I give money to someone who needs it, that's Islamic; when I give work to my friend who is unemployed, that is Islamic. So everything we do is Islamic. This is our vision, that when we do something that is good, this is Islamic."

Not all journalists are as conscious of the obligation to invite good and forbid evil as are *Republika* journalists and students of *dakwah* at Indonesia's Islamic universities and institutes. However, it is nevertheless a fundamental aspect of journalism in Indonesia, Malaysia, and probably other majority Muslim countries as well.

INDEPENDENCE WITHOUT LIBERALISM

What I learned from the journalism faculties at the Islamic universities and institutes thus confirmed that I was right, that Muslim journalists in Indonesia and Malaysia uphold the same basic principles of journalism—truth, verification, balance, independence from power—as do their Western counterparts, but the ways in which they explain these principles to themselves are different. In 1979, sociologist Herbert Gans wrote that the paraideology of American journalism was reform, a liberal set of values that grew out of the Progressive Era. Although most journalists in Indonesia and Malaysia endorse these same principles, the values on which they are based are not liberal. Instead, for many of the journalists who work in the newsrooms I have studied, good journalism is grounded in a specific set of values based on justice and the obligation to promote what is good and prevent what is evil. The struggle for justice and the protection of the weak is thus not only fundamental to Islam, it is also the overarching ideology of journalism in Indonesia and Malaysia.[4]

It is important to understand that Muslim journalists in Indonesia and Malaysia who reject the labels liberal and secular can at the same time promote both tolerance and democracy. Like political scientist Jeremy Menchik (2016, 3), who observed that "our understanding of the relationship between religion and the state outside of secular-liberal government is limited," I argue that our understanding of journalism has also been limited. What he has shown about the existence of tolerance without liberalism in the Muslim organizations Nahdlatul Ulama (NU) and Muhammadiyah has direct parallels with what can be found among pious journalists in both Indonesia and Malaysia. These journalists support independent media yet work for publications that, with the possible exceptions of *Malaysiakini* and *Tempo*, cannot be described as either secular or liberal. In Malaysia we see this nonliberal emphasis on justice and inviting good and prohibiting evil in *Harakah*'s scathing critiques of the greed of Malaysia's ruling Barisan Nasional (National Front) coalition. It is obvious in *Tempo*'s investigative reports on corruption, *Malaysiakini*'s coverage of the 1MDB scandal, and *Republika*'s preference for stories that showcase instances of tolerance. It is also apparent in *Sabili*'s exposés of unjust treatment of Muslims in the Palestinian territories and elsewhere in the world.

For much of Indonesian press history, "evil" was related to the political context of Soeharto's New Order—an unjust political system in which there were virtually no limits to the government's authority. This lack of justice led *Tempo* magazine writers to lend subtle support to ordinary men and women in their struggle against the power of the state (Steele 2005). It is well known that in New Order Indonesia, journalistic "professionalism" meant functioning as a mouthpiece for government programs and plans. It was not understood to mean challenging government authorities or otherwise acting as a watchdog in the style of Western media. The "Pancasila press" of the New Order was expected to be a partner in economic development (Romano 2003, 37–52).

As communication scholar Angela Romano (2003, 80) has noted, "Exposés on corruption, collusion and mismanagement were . . . often criticized for being negative, socially disruptive and damaging to public faith in the delicate and still-developing institutions of state. The ambivalence surrounding the journalists' role and the uncertainty about what issues were worth taking risks for thus emerged as enormous disincentives to intrepid journalism." *Tempo* magazine felt the wrath of the Soeharto administration when in 1994 it reported on a procurement scandal, thereby shining a light on disarray within the regime. During its underground period, *Sabili* experienced these same disincentives, choosing to focus on tyranny and the suffering of Muslims under any authoritarian regime other than the one at home. Today's journalists in Malaysia face many of these same challenges, as those who work for mainstream media find it easier simply to support the ruling coalition than risk harassment and legal action.

SAME GOAL, DIFFERENT PATHS

In Indonesia under President Soeharto, Islam offered both an alternative political ideology and a subtle means of opposing the regime, and the situation today in Malaysia is similar. Just as *Tempo*'s Arif Zulkifli was involved in the *tarbiyah* movement while at the University of Indonesia, both Zulkifli Sulong and Ahmad Lutfi Othman of *Harakah* were active in Islamic student associations in Malaysia, as was *Malaysiakini*'s Fathi Aris Omar. As Fathi said, "There is no other choice in Malaysia. There is PAS and UMNO. If you are going to be true to Islamic principles, there is no other choice." Starting out as an Islamic student activist, Fathi says his views began to change when he started to read in English, and to question what would happen after the implementation of the Islamic state. "The bottom line," he said, "is that Islam is trying to sell the rhetoric without giving the outline of what to do next. There is no concept, there is no policy."

While still a student, Fathi became friendly with Ahmad Lutfi Othman, who was at that time the editor of the campus section of *Harakah*. Fathi started to write for the paper, which he did off and on throughout the 1990s. The two became close and, inspired by the Indonesian student movement's success in toppling Soeharto, worked together on a series of newspapers and magazines. In 1998, when Lutfi established *Detik*, named after the magazine that had been banned in Indonesia four years earlier, Fathi joined him there. After the Malaysian Home Ministry refused to renew *Detik*'s permit in 1999, thereby shutting it down, Lutfi and Fathi formed a group of independent media activists called Kumpulan Aktivis Media Independent (KAMI). That same year, Fathi became involved with the *reformasi* movement, not so much because of his sympathy for Anwar Ibrahim as a leader but rather because of the feeling that the former deputy prime minister had been treated unjustly. He recalled that engaging with other young activists and learning more about democracy, human rights, and freedom of expression caused him to see things differently. "*Reformasi* changed me," he said. "We had not been exposed to human rights, debates, democracy, stuff like that. When I discovered these things, it was like, 'Why didn't they tell me earlier?'" In words that are strikingly similar to those used by Arif Zulkifli in Indonesia once he left the *tarbiyah* movement, Fathi said that he had learned that truth did not occupy one particular space. "I think there is an important difference between Islam and political Islam," Fathi added, "between Islam as a religion, and Islam as a political ideal."

Ultimately Fathi and Lutfi's paths diverged. Fathi joined the outwardly secular news portal *Malaysiakini* and Lutfi remained at *Harakah*, but their shared commitment to freedom of expression remained strong. When asked to explain the difference between himself and his friend, Fathi chose his words carefully. By the time he had joined *Malaysiakini*, Fathi said, "Lutfi was senior [at *Harakah*], where they have their own very strong belief in the Islamic understanding of the political process. I am still in the process of learning." When I asked Fathi if he believed in the Islamic state, he said, "I did believe, but when I was younger." The question now, Fathi said, is how to contextualize Islam: "We say we believe in Islam as a way of life, but how do you [implement] the Islamic way of life? There is no outline to say so. There is no clear-cut way. That is my thesis now."

The friendship between Lutfi and Fathi and the ties between *Harakah* and *Malaysiakini*—both to some degree inspired by developments in Indonesia— are just two examples of the connectivity of these two "*serumpun*" countries with common roots. Debate over the proper role of Islam in the modern state led to the *tarbiyah* movement that inspired *Sabili* and launched the Indonesian Prosperous Justice Party (Partai Keadilan Sejahtera, PKS), and at the same time influenced the Malaysian student activists who joined PAS, the political party that owns *Harakah*. Reaction to this debate from Indonesian neomodernist scholars like Nurcholish Madjid, who called for a renewal in Islamic thinking, appeared not only in ICMI-owned *Republika* newspaper

Ahmad Lutfi Othman and former *Malaysiakini* editor Fathi Aris Omar, 2013. Photo courtesy of *Harakah*.

but also the pages of the nonconfessional magazine *Tempo*. Similarly, the May 1998 toppling of Indonesia's Soeharto reverberated across the Straits of Malacca and, sparked by the sacking of charismatic former deputy prime minister Anwar Ibrahim, inspired *reformasi*. This pro-democracy movement launched a number of new blogs and web portals, the most famous of which was *Malaysiakini*. Like *Harakah*, *Malaysiakini* challenged the authority of the ruling coalition, albeit from a secular perspective. The five publications studied in this book are thus linked not only by the ways in which they relate to political Islam but also by their relationship to authoritarianism.

There are of course striking variations among these journalists as well as between the two countries where they reside. Some of these differences can be explained by such factors as the legacy of colonial rule, the development of the early nationalist press, the politicization of religion, the source of religious authority, and the role of the state. In Indonesia there is no one officially mandated way of understanding Islam, as the variety of views expressed by journalists from *Tempo*, *Republika*, and *Sabili* demonstrates. In Malaysia it is different, however, and the state is the expert. As *Malaysiakini's* Fathi said, Malaysia's problem is rigidity: "It is so black and white, it is a zero-sum game, there is no nuance in between."

Cultural theorist Stuart Hall's (2002, 26) definition of cosmopolitanism as "the ability to stand outside of having one's life written and scripted by any one community" is relevant to each of the publications I have described. The desire to "to navigate between outright secularism, bland traditionalism, and uncompromisingly literalist reinterpretations of Islamic teaching" (Kersten 2015) has been most obvious in the pages of *Tempo*, which has given space since its founding to such scholars as Nurcholish Madjid, Azyumardi Azra, and Gus Dur. Yet cosmopolitanism has also been evident in the pages of *Republika*, in the struggle of the "professionals" at *Harakah*, and among the Malay-Muslims at *Malaysiakini*, each of whom has had one foot in the Islamic tradition and the other in the modernities of the West. Even *Sabili's* counter-cosmopolitanism—as ardently opposed as it was to anything that smacked of secularism, liberalism, and pluralism—was not indifferent to this struggle.

Islam is not static, either in Indonesia and Malaysia or elsewhere. Changes in Muslim practices in Indonesia and Malaysia have been well-documented, and in both countries the approach of journalists to Islam is not what it was forty-five years ago when *Tempo* was founded. The deepening Islamization of the urban middle class has been obvious in both Malaysia and Indonesia, and outward signs of piety abound. Goenawan Mohamad, *Tempo's* founding editor, is skeptical of the newfound piety among Indonesian journalists, noting in 2009 that "the word Islamic is only a recent development. In the past, people like Mochtar Loebis and Rosihan Anwar, they didn't really talk about Islam." According to Goenawan, it's about justification: "When you talk to them about Islam, it's about justification," he said. Yet this may be precisely the point. As Goenawan said, Indonesian journalists justify their work in Islamic terms because it's their "language" and "treasure of values": "So [they] can be very at peace, peaceful with that. It's only how do you justify to yourself what you are doing? And people use religion, Islam, and in that sense, yes, Islam can be very useful. That's not because Islam inspired them. Islam is the language to justify what you believe in journalism."

Saptoni, the head of the Department of Communication Studies and an expert on Islamic jurisprudence at the UIN Sunan Kalijaga in Yogyakarta, disagrees with Goenawan's argument. He says that graduates of Islamic institutes and universities such as his do more than simply justify their work in the language of Islam. According to Saptoni, they are inspired by it. "The material that they learn in class isn't just journalism," he said, "but also the Qur'an, the Hadith, *fiqih*, etc. In practice, when they study journalism or when they go into the field and do practical work, what they have learned in class becomes an inspiration for them as they work."

Whether Islam justifies good journalism or inspires it, the story of the modern journalisms of Islam is thus what is familiar and liberal set off against the deeply Islamic. For Western policy makers who seek to engage with journalists in majority Muslim countries, an understanding of how the norms and values of journalism are understood within the context and culture of Islam is essential. In a world in which Islam is often described as opposed to democracy and pluralism, it is important to recognize that for many journalists who are neither "liberal" nor "secular," it is still possible to fight for justice and defend the rights of the weak. The goal of Muslim journalists to expose corruption among political elites may be the same as that of Western watchdog journalism, but the pathway there is different. This path is not a halfway point to the "real" way of doing journalism; it is instead how many Muslim professionals understand and explain their work.

The modern history of both Indonesia and Malaysia suggests that without independent media, justice is no more possible than either freedom or democracy. If Goenawan is right that the "treasure" of journalists is the language of Islam, then those who wish to engage with the Islamic world should consider using the local idiom to reach it. In some cases, Islam does constrain, but in others it inspires.

NOTES

INTRODUCTION

1   This duration has included every summer, semester break, and four Fulbright or sabbatical years since 1997.

2   "O believers . . . do not spy, neither backbite one another; would any of you like to eat the flesh of his dead brother? You would abominate it" (Qur'an, "Al-Hujuraat" 49:12). I am grateful to former journalist Ekky Imanjaya for pointing this out to me in personal correspondence (email, January 17, 2013.)

3   An additional factor in my choice of news organizations in Malaysia was ease of access. Although I have given lectures and conducted workshops at the *New Straits Times, Berita Harian, Utusan,* and *The Star* newspapers, each of these organizations is linked to the governing Barisan Nasional (National Front) coalition, and it was clear that as an American researcher, I would not be given the kind of freedom to observe daily news practices that I had at *Harakah* and *Malaysiakini.*

4   In August 2015 the "Erdogan" or "professional" faction of the party, including many of my sources at *Harakah,* withdrew from PAS and established a new political party called Parti Amanah Negara, or Amanah. *Amanah* is also the name of the party newspaper.

5   The word *conservative* is problematic here, as *Sabili* journalists would probably prefer to refer to themselves as "pure" or "literalist." Moreover, one might confuse *conservatism* with the traditionalism of Nahdlatul Ulama, which is more tolerant of a variety of religious traditions. Although I am aware of the problems with this terminology, I nevertheless argue that *Sabili* represents the politically conservative, antiliberal opposite of the liberal/progressive views given space in the pages of *Tempo.*

CHAPTER ONE

1   Each of these terms is controversial. I have chosen to use Liddle's term *scripturalist,* while acknowledging that it too is not entirely accurate. As former *Malaysiakini*

143

journalist Fauwaz Abdul Aziz has pointed out, "Scripturalist connotes 'like scrip-ture,' whereas Islam has at least several texts—the Qur'an, the Hadith, the body of decisions on which there is scholarly consensus—and there is some debate about the relative eminence/priority that each 'text' enjoys" (personal correspondence, August 3, 2016).

2   "Bali Blast Suspect Named 'Man of the Year' by Islamic Magazine," December 30, 2002, www.hvk.org/2002/1202/302.html.

3   Sociologist Hazem Kandill's (2015) description of the process by which the Muslim Brotherhood "cultivates" new brothers parallels almost exactly the way in which Arif Zulkifli described his experience with the *tarbiyah* movement at the University of Indonesia in the early 1990s.

4   In *Sabili*, February 4, 2010.

5   The Permit to Publish was subsequently renamed the Press Publication Enter-prise Permit (Surat Izin Usaha Penerbitan Pers, SIUPP) in the revised Press Law of 1982.

6   Email correspondence, July 13, 2015.

7   In *Sabili*, May 30, 2002. In May 2002, when the institute became accredited as a university, the name was changed from IAIN (State Islamic Institute) Syarif Hidayatullah Jakarta to UIN (State Islamic University) Syarif Hidayatullah Jakarta (Steele 2012).

8   Fawauz Abdul Aziz, "The Secularists' Crusade," *Malaysiakini*, November 21, 2008, www.malaysiakini.com/news/93506.

CHAPTER TWO

1   The 1981 fatwa forbids Muslims from attending Christian services and "suggests" that it is better not to extend Christmas greetings. The text of the fatwa can be found here: http://forum.detik.com/trit-petromax-teks-fatwa-mui-tahun-1981-ttg-perayaan -natal-t594754.html.

2   Masha 2012. Fieldwork for this study was conducted between May 1, 2012, and Janu-ary 31, 2013, with additional research in July 2014 and July 2016.

3   Editorial meeting, July 18, 2016.

4   The Ahmadiyah Muslim community is a movement within Islam that is considered devient by mainstream Sunni Muslims in both Indonesia and Malaysia.

5   *Tempo*'s Malela Mahargasarie, who later hired eighteen *Republika* journalists for the new *Koran Tempo* in 2001, had participated in some even earlier conversations with this group. Although he never left *Tempo*, he nevertheless respected the *Berita Buana/Republika* group as journalists.

6   In *Tempo*, January 9, 1993.

7   According to the news organization's own data, only 15.63 percent of *Republika Online*'s readers are women (see www.republika.co.id/page/about).

8   As reported in *Jakarta Globe*, January 12, 2012.

9   Multiple conversations in Jakarta confirmed this. I have yet to meet a single journalist who does not work for *Republika* who thinks that the newspaper was neutral in the 2014 presidential election.

10 Exceptions to this rule are photos in *Republika*'s sports section.

11 "MUI Tolak Larangan Khitan Perempuan" [MUI refuses the ban on female circumcision], *Republika*, January 22, 2013.

12 Meeting with *Republika* editors Ferry Kisihandi, E. H. Ismail, and Yogi Ardi, January 22, 2013.

13 "LGBT Ancaman Serius" [LGBT a serious threat], www.republika.co.id/berita /koran/halaman-1/16/01/24/o1gi281-lgbt-ancaman-serius.

14 Febriana Firdaus, "Forum LGBTIQ somasi Republika terkait artikel 'LGBT Ancaman Serius'" [LGBTIQ Forum summons *Republika* in connection with its article: "LGBT a serious threat"], www.rappler.com/indonesia/121324-komunitas-lgbtiq -somasi-republika. On June 9, 2016, the Press Council dismissed the *somasi*, finding that *Republika* had in subsequent editions "given enough space to those who represented LGBT groups." The Press Council urged LGBTIQ to use its right of reply. The Press Council's decision can be found at this link: Keputusan Dewan Pers 308/ KP-K/VI/2016.

15 "Dompet Dhuafa dan HU Republika: 'Merangkul Korban LGBT, Menolak Legalisasi LGBT,'" www.dompetdhuafa.org/post/detail/1827/dompet-dhuafa-dan-hu-republika— %E2%80%9Cmerangkul-korban-lgbt—menolak-legalisasi-lgbt%E2%80%9D.

16 During 2011, for example, Muhammadiyah celebrated Eid on August 30, whereas NU decided on August 31. *Republika* ultimately chose to go with the government's decision (NU's way), even though the general perception is that about 30 percent of newspaper's readers are Muhammadiyah and only 10 percent NU.

CHAPTER THREE

1   As Farish Noor (2014, 14) has noted, although not all of the positions taken by PAS make sense from a mechanistic or political perspective, they do make sense from an ideological or Islamist perspective. PAS leadership's support for a Hudud law is a good example of this.

2   As reported in *Malaysiakini*, June 5, 2015.

3   The article headlines are "Islam Asas Kekuatan PAS" and "Kezaliman belum berakhir," respectively.

4   I am grateful to Fauwaz Abdul Aziz for pointing out the significance of this distinction. See, for example, the December 13, 2013, Astro Awani story, "Mat Sabu denies Shia Links," http://english.astroawani.com/malaysia-news/mat-sabu-denies-shia -links-26909.

5   As a white, uncovered female foreigner, I have never been able to buy *Harakah* on the street, although I have been able to pay for a subscription to the e-paper at *Harakah*'s business office.

6   Zulkifli left *HarakahDaily.net* in July 2013, after having been with the *Harakah* organization for twenty-six years. When he moved to *The Malaysian Insider* as the editor of their "Bahasa Malaysia" section, he informed his managing director: "Please give me two years to join TMI, and if after two years you think *Harakah* still needs me, please call me back."

7   Nigel Aw, " PAS Youth reprimands Harakah, demands revamp," www.malaysiakini .com/news/214239.

8   Quoted in *Mingguan Malaysia*, December 13, 2015.

CHAPTER FOUR

1   Statistics for 2010 from the CIA's *World Factbook* state that Malaysia's population consists of 50.1 percent Malay, 22.6 percent Chinese, 11.8 percent indigenous, 6.7 percent Indian, 0.7 percent other, and 8.2 percent noncitizens; see "The World Factbook," www.cia.gov/library/publications/resources/the-world-factbook/geos/my.html.

2   *The Malaysian Insider*, which did report on the scandal, was shut down "for commercial reasons" in March 2016, a few weeks after it was blocked by the Malaysian Communications and Multimedia Commission as part of a crackdown on critical coverage. In July 2015, *The Edge* received a three-month suspension for its coverage of 1MDB, which was deemed a threat to public order and national security.

3   Here I'm drawing on anthropologist Michael Peletz's (2006, 310) definition of pluralism as "social fields, cultural domains, and more encompassing systems in which two or more principles, categories, groups, sources of authority, or ways of being in the world are not only present, tolerated, and accommodated but also *accorded legitimacy* in a basic Weberian sense" (emphasis in the original).

4   Despite severe headaches and his ongoing criticism of the ways in which Malaysian government authorities handle Ramadan, in subsequent years Shufiyan fasted for the entire month.

5   Investigative Reporters and Editors (IRE) defines investigative reporting as "the reporting, through one's own initiative and work product, of matters of importance to readers, viewers, or listeners. In many cases, the subjects of the reporting wish the matters under scrutiny to remain undisclosed." See "2016 IRE Awards FAQ," http://ire.org/awards/ire-awards/faq/#judgecrit.

6   Hazlan Zakaria, " 'Blue Monday' at Carcosa Seri Negara," *Malaysiakini*, March 21, 2011, www.malaysiakini.com/news/159278.

7   As quoted in Kuek Ser Kuang Keng, "Anwar: I'm Not the Man in the Sex Video," *Malaysiakini*, March 21, 2011, www.malaysiakini.com/news/159257.

8   Hafiz Yatim, "Spotlight on the Infamous 'Datuk T' Trio," *Malaysiakini*, March 26, 2011 www.malaysiakini.com/news/159729.

9   Kow Gah Chie, "Sex Video: Datuk T Trio Pleads Guilty, Fined RM5.500," *Malaysiakini*, June 24, 2011, www.malaysiakini.com/news/167883.

10   As quoted in Nigel Aw, "Azizah Thankful Public Can See through Sex Video," *Malaysiakini*, August 4, 2011, www.malaysiakini.com/news/171934.

11 As quoted in "Imam Flings Shoes at Judges over Eviction Case," *Malaysiakini*, February 22, 2012, www.malaysiakini.com/news/189968.

12 Ibid.

13 Ibid.

14 As quoted in "Shoe-throwing Imam Jailed One Year for Contempt," *Malaysiakini*, March 8, 2012, www.malaysiakini.com/news/191441.

15 Email to *Malaysiakini* editorial, March 8, 2012.

16 The actual words spoken are "Bismillah hir rahmanir rahhim" (In the name of Allah, the most gracious and compassionate). I am grateful to Amira Firdaus for her help in further explaining the implications of Hazlan's statement.

CHAPTER FIVE

1 *Manikebu* means "buffalo sperm."

2 Goenawan Mohamad disputes this, saying that Syu'bah Asa was "not involved" in Mukti Ali's group, although he may have "had some sympathy."

3 The introductory edition of *Tempo* contained this definition of good journalism. It was written by Goenawan Mohamad and has been reprinted many times. "Our journalism will not be one-sided, or based on the politics of a single group. We believe that neither virtue nor the lack of virtue is the monopoly of any one side. We believe that the duty of the press is not to spread prejudice, but rather to wipe it out, not to sow the seeds of hatred, but rather to communicate mutual understanding. The journalism of this magazine will not be sneering or insulting, obsequious or slavish. What gives us jurisdiction is not power or money, but rather good intentions, a sense of justice, and healthy thinking—all of which will be the basic philosophy of this magazine" (quoted in Steele 2005, 69).

4 Ulil pointed out the similarity between the use of the term *sepilis* to describe JIL and the term *Manikebu* to describe the signers of the *Manifes Kebudayaan* (Cultural manifesto).

CONCLUSION

1 According to details published in *Tempo*, September 22, 1984.

2 From *Encyclopedia Britannica* online, "Isnad," www.britannica.com/EBchecked/topic/296158/isnad.

3 I chose these four universities because of their size, prestige, and location. There are six UIN in Indonesia, four of them located on the Island of Java. UIN Syarif Hidayatullah Jakarta is the biggest of all the Islamic universities; UIN Sunan Kalijaga Yogyakarta, located in Central Java, is the nation's oldest and the third largest. UIN Sunan Gunung Djati Bandung is in West Java. IAIN Sunan Ampel is the largest of the state institutes for Islamic studies and is situated in Surabaya, the administrative center of East Java. It also aspires to be accredited as a state Islamic university.

4   And of course even the concept of "justice" is culture-bound. Although the US Constitution guarantees "fairness," meaning that the legal process must meet certain standards, it doesn't guarantee "justice"—or that the right outcome will be achieved. Fairness is secular, and it is all that can be guaranteed in a secular state. Justice is absolute right or wrong, and it is something we can only expect from a higher power. I am grateful to Jerry Macdonald for this insight.

BIBLIOGRAPHY

Abbot, Jason P. 2011. "Electoral Authoritarianism and the Print Media in Malaysia: Measuring Political Bias and Analyzing Its Cause." *Asian Affairs: An American Review* 38: 1–38.

Abbot, Jason P., and Oliver S. Franks. 2007. "Malaysia at Fifty: Conflicting Definitions of Citizenship." *Asian Affairs* 38 (3): 337–56.

Abror, Dhimam. 2009. Interview, Surabaya. June 6.

———. 2015. Interview, Surabaya. March 7.

Abshar-Abdallah, Ulil. 2000. Interview, Jakarta. January 4.

———. 2002. "Menyegarkan Kembali Pemahaman Islam" [Reinvigorating Islamic understanding]. *Kompas*, November 11. http://islamlib.com/?site=1&aid=297&cat=content&cid=11&title=menyegarkan-kembali-pemahaman-islam.

———. 2015. Interview, Jakarta. January 6.

Abushouk, Ahmed Ibrahim. 2007. "Al-Manar and the Hadhrami Elites in the Malay World: Challenges and Prospects." *Journal of the Royal Asiatic Society* 17 (3): 301–22.

Ahmad, Dzulkefli. 2015. Interview, Shah Alam. June 5.

Ali, Muhamad. 2005. "The Rise of the Liberal Islam Network (JIL) in Contemporary Indonesia." *American Journal of Islamic Social Sciences* 22 (1): 1–26.

Alimah. 2012. "Konstrucksi Wacana Anti-Ahmadiyah di Indonesia (Analisis Wacana Kritis Berita tentang Ahmadiyah di Harian Umum *Republika* dan Majalah *Sabili* Tahun 1993–2011) [Construction of Anti-Ahmadiyah discourse in Indonesia (critical discourse analysis of news stories about Ahmadiyah in *Republika* newspaper and *Sabili* magazine 1993–2011]. Master's thesis, Paramadina Graduate Schools.

Amin, Hussein. 2002. "Freedom as a Value in Arab Media: Perceptions and Attitudes among Journalists." *Political Communication* 19 (2): 125–35.

An-Na'im, Abdullahi Ahmed. 2008. *Islam and the Secular State: Negotiating the Future of Shari'a*. Cambridge, MA: Harvard University Press.

Anam, Faris Khairul. 2009. *Fikih Jurnalistik: Etika and Kebebasan Pers Menurut Islam* [Journalistic jurisprudence: Ethics and press freedom according to Islam]. Jakarta: Pustaka Al-Kautsar.

Anwar, Zainah. 2001. "What Islam, Whose Islam"? In *The Politics of Multiculturalism: Pluralism and Citizenship in Malaysia, Singapore, and Indonesia*, edited by Robert W. Hefner, 227–52. Honolulu: University of Hawai'i Press.

Appiah, Kwame Anthony. 2006. *Cosmopolitanism: Ethics in a World of Strangers*. New York: W. W. Norton & Company.

Armando, Ade. 2013. Interview, Jakarta. January 27.

Armstrong, Karen. 2002. *Islam: A Short History*. New York: Random House.

Arnakim, Lili Yulyadi. 2011. "The Impact of Islamic Awakening on Indonesian Foreign Policy, 1993–2004." PhD diss., University of Malaya.

Asa, Syu'bah. 2000. Interview, Jakarta. August 2.

Aslan, Reza. 2005. *No God But God: The Origins, Evolution, and Future of Islam*. London: Arrow Books.

Assyaukanie, Luthfi. 2009. *Islam and the Secular State in Indonesia*. Singapore: Institute of Southeast Asian Studies.

Astraatmadja, Atmakusumah. 2009. Interview, Jakarta. August 28.

Aziz, Fauwaz Abdul. 2007. Interview, Kuala Lumpur. August 11.

———. 2008. Interview, Kuala Lumpur. December 22.

Azra, Azyumardi. 1992. "The Transmission of Islamic Reformism to Indonesia: Networks of Middle Eastern and Malay-Indonesian 'Ulama' in the Seventeenth and Eighteenth Centuries." PhD diss., Columbia University, New York.

———. 1999. "The Transmission of *al-Manar*'s Reformism to the Malay-Indonesian World: The Cases of *al-Imam* and *al-Munir*." *Studia Islamika* 6 (3): 75–100.

———. 2014. Interview, Ciputat. August 14.

Bailyn, Bernard. 1967. *The Ideological Origins of the American Revolution*. Cambridge, MA: Harvard University Press.

Bektiati, Bina. 2009. Interview, Jakarta. July 23.

Benda, Harry J. 1958. *The Crescent and the Rising Sun: Indonesian Islam under the Japanese Occupation, 1942–1945*. The Hague: W. van Hoeve Ltd.

Bertrand, Jacques. 2010. "Political Islam and Democracy in the Majority Muslim Country of Indonesia." In *Islam and Politics in Southeast Asia*, edited by Johan Saravanamuttu, 45–64. New York: Routledge.

bin Ibrahim, Azmuddin. 2012. Interview, Selangor. December 20.

Brown, Graham. 2005. "The Rough and Rosy Road: Sites of Contestation in Malaysia's Shackled Media Industry." *Pacific Affairs* 78: 39–56.

Bubalo, Anthony, and Greg Fealy. 2005. *Joining the Caravan? The Middle East, Islamism, and Indonesia*. Alexandria, Australia: Longueville Media for the Lowry Institute for International Policy Double Bay.

Budiman, Arief. 1999. Interview, Jakarta. December 6.

Burhani, Ahmad Najib. 2013. "The Struggle for the Face of Reformist Islam in Indonesia." In *Contemporary Developments in Indonesian Islam: Explaining the "Conservative Turn,"* edited by Martin Van Brunissen, 104–44. Singapore: Institute for Southeast Asian Studies.

Case, William. 2011. *Executive Accountability in Southeast Asia: The Role of Legislatures in New Democracies and under Electoral Authoritarianism.* Honolulu: East-West Center.

Chandran, Premesh. 2008. Interview, Kuala Lumpur. March 26.

Chin, James. 2003. "Malaysiakini and Its Impact on Journalism and Politics in Malaysia." In *Asia.com: Asia Encounters the Internet,* edited by Kong Chong Ho, Randy Kluver, and Kenneth C. C. Yang, 129–42. London: RoutledgeCurzon.

Chusjairi, Juni Alfiah. 2014. "The Construction of an Anti-Western Islamist Discourse in Indonesian Magazines." PhD diss., University of Western Sydney.

Cook, Michael. 2003. *Forbidding Wrong in Islam.* Cambridge: Cambridge University Press.

Crouch, Harold. 1988. *The Army and Politics in Indonesia.* Revised edition. Ithaca, NY: Cornell University Press.

———. 1996. *Government and Society in Malaysia.* Ithaca, NY: Cornell University Press.

Damhuri, Elba. 2012a. Interview, Jakarta. June 4.

———. 2012b. Interview, Jakarta. June 5.

———. 2012c. Interview, Jakarta. June 6.

Daulay, Hamdan, Rifa'I, Akhmad, and Musthofa. 2006. *Jurnalistik.* Yogyakarta, Indonesia: UIN Sunan Kalijaga.

de Burgh, Hugo, ed. 2005. "Introduction." In *Making Journalists: Diverse Models, Global Issues,* 1–18. New York: Routledge.

Dhume, Sadanand. 2009. *My Friend the Fanatic: Travels with a Radical Islamist.* New York: Skyhorse Publishing.

Dick, Howard. 1990. "Further Reflections on the Middle Class." In *The Politics of Middle Class Indonesia,* edited by Richard Tanter and Kenneth Young, 63–70. Clayton, Victoria: Monash University, Centre of Southeast Asian Studies.

Dueze, Mark. 2006. "Global Journalism Education: A Conceptual Approach." *Journalism Studies* 7 (1): 19–34.

El Fikri, Syahruddin. 2010. "Etika peliputan jurnalistik dan penulisan feature" [Ethics of journalistic reporting and feature writing]. Unpublished manuscript.

———. 2010. Interview, Jakarta. October 15.

El Shirazy, Habiburrahman. 2004. *Ayat-Ayat Cinta* [Verses of love]. Semarang: Pesantren Karya Basmala, Jakarta: Republika.

Eliraz, Giora. 2008. "Distinctive Contemporary Voices: Liberal Islamic Thought in Indonesia." *Studia Islamika* 15 (3): 379–416.

Ettema, James S., and Theodore L. Glasser. 1998. *Custodians of Conscience: Investigative Journalism and Public Virtue.* New York: Columbia University Press.

Feith, Herbert, and Lance Castles, eds. 1970. *Indonesian Political Thinking 1945–1965.* Ithaca, NY: Cornell University Press.

Galandar, Mahmoud. 2008. "Communication in the Early Muslim Society." In *Media and Muslim Society,* edited by Mohamed Yusuf Hossain, 45–71. Kuala Lumpur: International Islamic University.

Gan, Steven. 2008. Interview, Kuala Lumpur. March 24.

———. 2009. Interview, Kuala Lumpur. July 2.

———. 2016. Interview, Kuala Lumpur. July 2.

Gans, Herbert. 1979. *Deciding What's News: A Study of CBS Evening News, NBC Nightly News, Newsweek, and Time*. New York: Pantheon.

George, Cherian. 2006. *Contentious Journalism and the Internet: Towards Democratic Discourse in Malaysia and Singapore*. Singapore: Singapore University Press.

Gomez, Edmund Terrence. 2004. "Politics of the Media Business." In *Reflections: The Mahathir Years*, edited by Bridget Welsh, 475–85. Washington, DC: Southeast Asian Studies Program (SAIS).

Hadad, Toriq. 2009. Interview, Jakarta. June 5.

"Hadi and Company Complete Clean Sweep." 2015. *Malaysiakini*, June 5. www.malaysiakini.com/news/300765.

Hall, Stuart. 2002. "Political Belonging in a World of Multiple Identities." In *Conceiving Cosmopolitanism: Theory, Context, and Practice*, edited by Steven Vertovec and Robin Cohen, 25–31. Oxford: Oxford University Press.

Hanitzsch, Thomas. 2005. "Journalists in Indonesia: Educated but Timid Watchdogs." *Journalism Studies* 6 (4): 493–508.

Hannerz, Ulf. 1990. "Cosmopolitans and Locals in World Culture." *Theory, Culture, and Society* 7: 237–51.

Harymurti, Bambang. 2000. Interview, Jakarta. January 21.

———. 2012. Interview, Jakarta. December 31.

Hefner, Robert W. 1993. "Islam, Class, and Civil Society: ICMI and the Struggle for the Indonesian Middle Class." *Indonesia* 56 (October): 1–35.

———. 1997a. "Introduction." In *Islam in an Era of Nation States: Politics and Religious Revival in Muslim Southeast Asia*, edited by Robert W. Hefner and Patricia Horvatich, 3–40. Honolulu: University of Hawai'i Press.

———. 1997b. "Print Islam: Mass Media and Ideological Rivalries among Indonesian Muslims." *Indonesia* 64 (October): 77–103.

———. 2000. *Civil Islam: Muslims and Democratization in Indonesia*. Princeton, NJ: Princeton University Press.

———. 2008. "Introduction: Civic Platforms or Radical Springboards?" In *Muslim Professional Associations and Politics in Southeast Asia*, edited by Robert W. Hefner and Patricia Horvatich, 3–16. Seattle: National Bureau of Asian Research.

Heryanto, Ariel. 2011. "Upgraded Piety and Pleasure." In *Islam and Popular Culture in Indonesia and Malaysia*, edited by Andrew N. Weintraub, 60–82. London: Routledge.

Heryanto, Ariel, and Sumit K. Mandal. 2003. *Challenging Authoritarianism in Southeast Asia: Comparing Indonesia and Malaysia*. London: RoutledgeCurzon.

Hill, David T. 1994. *The Press in New Order Indonesia*. Jakarta: Pustaka Sinar Harapan.

Hill, David T., and Krishna Sen, eds. 2011. *Politics and the Media in Twenty-First-Century Indonesia: Decade of Democracy*. London: Routledge.

Hilman, Arys. 2012. Interview, Jakarta. May 11.

Hollinger, David. 2002. "Not Universalists, Not Pluralists: The New Cosmopolitans Find Their Own Way." In *Conceiving Cosmopolitanism: Theory, Context, and Practice*, edited by Steven Vertovec and Robin Cohen, 227–39. Oxford: Oxford University Press.

Hooker, M. B. 2003. *Notes on Indonesian Islam: Social Change through Contemporary Fatwa*. Sydney: Allen and Unwin; Honolulu: University of Hawai'i Press.

Howard, Philip N. 2011. *The Digital Origins of Dictatorship and Democracy: Information Technology and Political Islam*. New York: Oxford University Press.

Hume, Ellen. 2007. *University Journalism Education: A Global Challenge*. Washington, DC: Center for International Media Assistance and National Endowment for Democracy.

Hwang, Julie Chernov. 2010. "When Parties Swing: Islamist Parties and Institutional Moderation in Malaysia and Indonesia." *Southeast Asia Research* 18 (4): 635–74.

Ichwan, Moch Nur. 2013. "Towards a Puritanical Moderate Islam: The Majelis Ulama Indonesia and the Politics of Religious Orthodoxy." In *Contemporary Developments in Indonesian Islam: Explaining the "Conservative Turn,"* edited by Martin van Bruinessen, 60–104. Singapore: Institute of Southeast Asian Studies.

Ilaihi, Wahyu. 2010. *Komunikasi Dakwah* [*Dakwah* communication]. Bandung: PT Remaja Rosdakarya.

Ilaihi, Wahyu, and Harjani Hefni. 2007. *Pengantar Sejarah Dakwah* [An introduction to the history of *dakwah*]. Jakarta: Kencana.

Irawanto, Budi. 2011. "Riding Waves of Change: Islamic Press in Post-authoritarian Indonesia." In *Politics and Media in Twenty-first Century Indonesia: Decade of Democracy*, edited by Krishna Sen and David Hill, 67–84. New York: Routledge.

"Islam Kosmopolitan Dalam Berita" [Cosmopolitan Islam in the news]. 1993. *Tempo*, January 9.

"Islam Punya Konsep Kenegaraan?" [Does Islam have a concept of the state?]. 1984. *Tempo*, December 29.

Jomo, Kwame Sundaram, and Ahmed Shabery Cheek. 1988. "The Politics of Malaysia's Islamic Resurgence." *Third World Quarterly* 10 (2): 843–68.

———. 1992. "Malaysia's Islamic Movements." In *Fragmented Vision: Culture and Politics in Contemporary Malaysia*, edited by Joel S. Kahn and Francis Loh Kok Wah, 79–106. Honolulu: University of Hawai'i Press.

Junaidi, Irfan. 2016. Interview, Jakarta. July 13.

Kahn, Joel S. 2006. *Other Malays: Nationalism and Cosmopolitanism in the Modern Malay World*. Honolulu: Asian Studies Association of Australia in association with University of Hawai'i Press.

Kamali, Mohammad Hashim. 1998. *Freedom of Expression in Islam*. Kuala Lumpur: Ilmiah Publishers.

———. 2002. *Freedom, Equality, and Justice in Islam*. Kuala Lumpur: Ilmiah Publishers.

Kandill, Hazem. 2015. *Inside the Brotherhood*. Cambridge, UK: Polity Press.

Keller, Anett. 2009. *Tantangan dari Dalam: Otonomi Redaksi di 4 Media Cetak Nasional; Kompas, Koran Tempo, Media Indonesia, Republika* [Challenge from inside: Editorial autonomy at 4 national print media; *Kompas, Koran Tempo, Media Indonesia, Republika*]. Jakarta: Friedrich Ebert Stiftung.

Kersten, Carool. 2009. "Islam, Cultural Hybridity, and Cosmopolitanism: New Muslim Intellectuals on Globalization." *Journal of International and Global Studies* 1 (1): 90–113.

———. 2015. *Islam in Indonesia: The Contest for Society, Ideas, and Values*. New York: Oxford University Press.

Khiabany, Gholam. 2006. "Religion and Media in Iran: The Imperative of the Market and the Straightjacket of Islamism." *Westminster Papers in Communication and Culture* 3 (2): 3–21.

Kholili, H. M. 2011. Interview, Yogyakarta. August 2.

Kopal, Indrani. 2010. Interview, Kuala Lumpur. August 18.

Kovach, Bill, and Tom Rosenstiel. 2001. *The Elements of Journalism: What Newspeople Should Know and the Public Should Expect*. New York: Three Rivers Press.

Koya, Abdar Rahman. 2013. Interview, Kuala Lumpur. December 26.

Laffan, Michael. 2003. "The Tangled Roots of Islamist Activism in Southeast Asia." *Cambridge Review of International Affairs* 16 (October): 397–414.

LaMay, Craig. 2007. *Exporting Press Freedom*. New Brunswick, NJ: Transaction Publishers.

Latif, Subky. 2015. Interview, Kuala Lumpur. June 15.

Lerner, Daniel. 2000 [1958]. "The Passing of Traditional Society." In *From Modernization to Globalization: Perspectives on Development and Social Change,* edited by J. Timmons Roberts and Amy Bellone, 119–33. 1958 edition published by Free Press. Oxford: Blackwell Publishers.

Levy, Leonard. 1985. *The Emergence of a Free Press*. New York: Oxford University Press.

Lewis, Bernard. 1988. *The Political Language of Islam*. Chicago: University of Chicago Press.

Liddle, William R. 1996a. "The Islamic Turn in Indonesia: A Political Explanation." *Journal of Asian Studies* 55 (2): 613–34.

———. 1996b. *Leadership and Culture in Indonesian Politics*. Sydney: Allen and Unwin.

Lim, Merlyna. 2005. *Islamic Radicalism and Anti-Americanism in Indonesia: The Role of the Internet*. Washington, DC: East-West Center Washington.

Liow, Joseph Chinyong. 2003. "'Visions of Serumpun': Tun Abdul Razak and the Golden Years of Indo-Malay Blood Brotherhood, 1967–75." *South East Asia Research* 11 (3): 327–50.

———. 2009. *Piety and Politics: Islamism in Contemporary Malaysia*. Oxford: Oxford University Press.

———. 2011. "Creating Cadres: Mobilization, Activism, and the Youth Wing of the Pan-Malaysian Islamic Party, PAS." *Pacific Affairs* 84 (4): 665–86.

Loebis, Amarzan. 2009. Interview, Jakarta. May 26.

Loh, Deborah. 2010. "Why Fast during Ramadan If One Is Non-Muslim?" *The Nut Graph*. August 19. www.thenutgraph.com/why-fast-during-ramadan-if-one-is-non -muslim/.

Madinier, Rémy. 2015. *Islam and Politics in Indonesia: The Masyumi Party between Democracy and Integralism*. Translated by Jeremy Desmond. Singapore: NUS Press.

Mahargasarie, Malela. 2012. Interview, Jakarta. December 26.

Mahmood, Saba. 2009. "Religious Reason and Secular Affect: An Incommensurable Divide?" *Critical Inquiry* 35 (summer): 836–62.

Malek, Zulkifly Abdul. 2011. "From Cairo to Kuala Lumpur: The Influence of the Egyptian Muslim Brotherhood on the Muslim Youth Movement of Malaysia (ABIM)." Master's thesis. Georgetown University, Washington, DC.

Masha, Nasihin. 2012. Interview, Jakarta. June 4.

———. 2014. Interview, Jakarta. July 7.

Mashuri, Ikhwanul Kiram. 2013. Interview, Jakarta. January 9.

Menchik, Jeremy. 2016. *Islam and Democracy in Indonesia: Tolerance without Liberalism*. New York: Cambridge University Press.

"Menghadapi Ide Pembaruan Islam" [Confronting the Islamic renewal of ideas]. 1973. *Tempo*, January 13.

Mohamad, Goenawan. 2009. Interview, Jakarta. September 3.

———. 2013. Interview, Jakarta. May 25.

———. 2015. Interview, Jakarta. January 1.

Mowlana, Hamid. 1993. "The New Global Order and Cultural Ecology." *Media Culture and Society* 15: 9–27.

———. 2003. "Foundation of Communication in Islamic Societies." In *Mediating Religion: Conversations in Media, Religion, and Culture*, edited by Jolyon Mitchell and Sophia Marriage, 305–16. London: T&T Clark.

Muhammad, Agus. 2001. "Jihad Lewat Tulisan" [Jihad via writing]. *Pantau*. July 22.

"MUI Tolak Larangan Khitan Perempuan" [MUI refuses the ban on female circumcision]. 2013. *Republika*, January 22.

Mulyatman, Eman. 2013. Interview, Jakarta. March 21.

———. 2015. Interview, Jakarta. July 3.

Munhanif, Ali. 1996. "Islam and the Struggle for Religious Pluralism in Indonesia: A Political Reading of the Religious Thought of Mukti Ali." *Studia Islamika* 3 (1): 79–126.

Muttaqin, Zainal. 2012. Interview, Jakarta. April 5.

Nada, Youssef, and Douglas Thompson. 2012. *Inside the Muslim Brotherhood*. London: Metro Publishing.

Nagota, Judith. 2010. "Authority and Democracy in Malaysian and Indonesian Islamic Movements." In *Islam and Politics in Southeast Asia*, edited by Johan Saravanamuttu, 18–44. New York: Routledge.

Nain, Zahoram. 2002. "The Media and Malaysia's *Reformasi* Movement." In *Media Fortunes Changing Times: Asean States in Transition*, edited by Russell H. K. Heng, 119–37. Singapore: Institute for Southeast Asian Studies.

Naipaul, V. S. 1982. *Among the Believers: An Islamic Journey*. New York: Vintage Books.

Nasr, Seyyed Hossein. 2002. *The Heart of Islam: Enduring Values for Humanity*. New York: HarperCollins.

Nasrul, Erdy. 2009. "Ormas Islam Di Persimpangan Jalan" [Islamic organizations at the crossroads]. *Sabili*, December 24.

"Nilai Mudharat Celana Jeans" [Jeans harm values]. 2010. *Sabili*, February 4.

Noor, Farish. 2014. *Islamism in a Mottled Nation: The Story of PAS*. Amsterdam: Amsterdam University Press.

Nurdi, Herry. 2009. Interview, Jakarta. August 31.

———. 2010. "Strategy Baru Pemurtadan" [New strategies for apostasy]. *Sabili*, January 7.

———. 2011. Interview, Jakarta. January 6.

———. 2014. Interview, Jakarta. March 25.

Nurdin, Ahmad Ali. 2005. "Islam and State: A Study of the Liberal Islamic Network in Indonesia, 1999–2004." *New Zealand Journal of Asian Studies* 7 (2): 20–39.

Nurzaman, Asep K. 2012. Interview, Jakarta. June 6.

Nussbaum, Martha. 1994. "Patriotism and Cosmopolitanism." *Boston Review*, October 1. http://bostonreview.net/martha-nussbaum-patriotism-and-cosmopolitanism.

Oemar, Priyantono. 2011. Interview, Jakarta. August 23.

Omar, Fathi Aris. 2009. Interview, Kuala Lumpur. July 16.

———. 2013. Interview, Kuala Lumpur. July 25.

Osman, Mohamed Nawab Bin Mohamed. 2011. "Transnational Islamism and Its Impact in Malaysia and Indonesia." *Middle East Review of International Affairs* 15 (2): 42–52.

Othman, Ahmad Lutfi. 2013a. Interview, Kuala Lumpur. July 2.

———. 2013b. Interview, Kuala Lumpur. July 25.

———. 2013c. Interview, Kuala Lumpur. December 23.

———. 2015a. Interview, Kuala Lumpur. June 9.

———. 2015b. Interview, Kuala Lumpur. December 22.

Pardini, Agung, n.d. "Majalah *Sabili*: Media Revivalis Gerakan Tarbiyah." [*Sabili* magazine: Revivalist media of the Tarbiyah movement]. www.scribd.com/doc/15912915/Majalah-Sabili-Media-Revivalis-Sejarah.

Pareanom, Yusi Avianto. 2009. Interview, Jakarta. July 23.

Parjitno, Subagio Budi. 2012. Interview, Bandung. October 18.

Peletz, Michael G. 2002. "Islam and the Cultural Politics of Legitimacy: Malaysia in the Aftermath of September 11." In *Muslim Politics: Pluralism, Contestation, Democratization*, edited by Robert Hefner, 240–72. Princeton, NJ: Princeton University Press.

———. 2006. "Transgenderism and Gender Pluralism in Southeast Asia since Early Modern Times." *Current Anthropology* 47: 309–40.

Pintak, Lawrence. 2013. "Islam, Identity, and Professional Values: A Study of Journalists in Three Muslim-Majority Regions." *Journalism: Theory, Practice, and Criticism* 15 (4): 482–503.

Pintak, Lawrence, and Jeremy Ginges. 2008. "The Mission of Arab Journalism: Creating Change in a Time of Turmoil." *International Journal of Press/Politics* 13 (3): 193–227.

Pintak, Lawrence, and Budi Setiyono. 2011. "The Mission of Indonesian Journalism: Balancing Democracy, Development, and Islamic Values." *International Journal of Press/Politics* 16 (2): 185–209.

Priyambodo, Daru. 2013. Interview, Jakarta. January 2.

Razak, Aidila. 2010. Interview, Kuala Lumpur. August 17.

Rezkisari, Indira. 2012. Interview, Jakarta. June 8.

Rijal, Syamsul. 2005. "Media and Islamism in Post–New Order Indonesia: The Case of *Sabili*." *Studia Islamika* 12 (3): 421–74.

Rizal, Yos. 2013. Interview, Jakarta. May 25.

Robison, Richard. 1996. "The Middle Class and the Bourgeoisie in Indonesia." In *The New Rich in Asia: Mobile Phones, McDonalds, and Middle-class Revolution*, edited by Richard Robison and David S. G. Goodman, 79–101. London: Routledge.

Roff, William R. 1967. *The Origins of Malay Nationalism*. New Haven, CT: Yale University Press.

———. 2009. *Studies on Islam and Society in Southeast Asia*. Singapore: NUS Press.

Romano, Angela. 2003. *Politics and the Press in Indonesia: Understanding an Evolving Political Culture*. London: RoutledgeCurzon.

Roy, Olivier. 2004. *Globalized Islam: The Search for a New Ummah*. New York: Columbia University Press.

Rubin, Barry, ed. 2010. *The Muslim Brotherhood*. New York: St. Martin's Press.

Ruslan, Heri. 2012. Interview, Jakarta. December 28.

Ruspiyandy, Deffy. 2013. "Umat Islam Jawa Barat Istiqomah Membasmi Sepilis" [Muslims of West Java eradicate *sepilis*]. *Sabili*. January 24.

Saat, Norshahril. 2012. "Islamising Malayness: *Ulama* Discourse and Authority in Contemporary Malaysia." *Contemporary Islam* 6: 135–53.

Sadewo, Joko. 2012. Interview, Jakarta. June 5.

———. 2014. Interview, Jakarta. July 7.

Sampasivam, Vicknésan. 2010. Interview, Kuala Lumpur. August 19.

Saptoni, 2011. Interview, Yogyakarta. August 3.

Satria, Adhes. 2009. "Olok-olok di Komunitas Liberal" [Ridicule in the liberal community]. *Sabili*. December 24.

———. 2010a. "Adu Strategi Lawan Kristenisasi" [Counterstrategies against Christianization]. *Sabili* January 7.

———. 2010b. "Kasak-Kusuk Ateis: Awas Komunis Bangkit Lagi" [Atheist intrigue: Beware Communism is rising again]. *Sabili*, March 4.

Satria, Adhes, and Daniel Handoko. 2010. "Rekayasa Menumbangkan Negeri Islam Terbesar" [Plot to topple the biggest Islamic country]. *Sabili*, January 21.

Scott, James C. 1985. *Weapons of the Weak: Everyday Forms of Peasant Resistance*. New Haven, CT: Yale University Press.

"Sebuah Masa Yang Berubah Sebuah Agama Yang Ramah" [A changing era and a friendly religion] and "Nurcholish Yang Menarik Gerbong" [Nurcholish who pulls the train]. 1986. *Tempo*, June 14.

Seib, Phillip. 2008. *The Al Jazeera Effect: How the New Global Media Are Reshaping World Politics*. Washington, DC: Potomac Books.

Shahab, Idrus F. 2009. Interview, Jakarta. October 5.

Sholihin, Burhan. 2013. Interview, Jakarta. January 2.

Shukur, Shufiyan, 2010. Interview, Kuala Lumpur. August 18.

Simon, Joel. 2014. *The New Censorship: Inside the Global Battle for Media Freedom.* New York: Columbia University Press.

Steele, Janet. 2005. *Wars Within: The Story of Tempo, an Independent Magazine in Soeharto's Indonesia.* Jakarta: Equinox Publishing and ISEAS.

———. 2006. "The Triumph of Moderation." *Foreign Policy.* www.foreignpolicy.com /articles/2006/01/04/the_triumph_of_moderation.

———. 2009. "Professionalism Online: How *Malaysiakini* Challenges Authoritarianism." *International Journal of Press/Politics* 14: 91–111.

———. 2011. "Justice and Journalism: Islam and Journalistic Values in Indonesia and Malaysia." *Journalism: Theory, Practice, and Criticism* 12 (June): 533–49.

———. 2012. "Journalism and 'the Call to Allah': Teaching Journalism in Indonesia's Islamic Universities and State Institutes." *International Journal of Communication* 6: 2944–61.

———. 2014. "Ramadan in the Newsroom: *Tempo, Malaysiakini,* and the State." In *Religious Pluralism, State, and Society in Asia,* edited by Chiara Formici, 197–215. London: Routledge.

Steenbrink, Karel A. 1999. "The Pancasila Ideology and an Indonesian Muslim Theology of Religions." In *Muslim Perceptions of Other Religions: A Historical Survey,* edited by Jacques Waardenburg, 280–96. New York: Oxford University Press.

Subhan, Arief. 2011. Interview, Ciputat. August 24.

Subroto. 2012. Interview, Jakarta. June 8.

Sulong, Zulkifli. 2013a. Interview, Kuala Lumpur. February 20.

———. 2013b. Interview, Kuala Lumpur. July 25.

———. 2014. Interview, Kuala Lumpur. December 24.

———. 2015. Interview, Kuala Lumpur. June 9.

Tagliacozzo, Eric, ed. 2009. *Southeast Asia and the Middle East: Islam, Movement, and the Longue Durée.* Singapore: NUS Press.

Tandoc, Edson C. 2014. "Journalism Is Twerking? How Web Analytics Is Changing the Process of Gatekeeping." *New Media and Society* 16 (4): 559–75.

Tamimi, Lutfi. 2014. Interview, Jakarta. January 3.

Tapsell, Russ. 2015. "Indonesia's Media Oligarchy and the 'Jokowi Phenomenon.'" *Indonesia* 99 (April): 29–50.

Tarrant, Bill. 2008. *Reporting Indonesia: The Jakarta Post Story 1983–2008.* Jakarta: Equinox Publishing.

Taufik, Ahmad. 2009. Interview, Jakarta. July 23.

Thohir, Erick. 2013. Interview, Jakarta. February 1.

Tomlinson, John. 1999. *Globalization and Culture.* Chicago: University of Chicago Press.

Tomsa, Dirk. 2012. "Moderating Islamism in Indonesia: Tracing Patterns of Party Change in the Prosperous Justice Party." *Political Research Quarterly* 65 (3): 486–98.

Tuchman, Gaye. 1972. "Objectivity as Strategic Ritual: An Examination of Newsmen's Notions of Objectivity." *American Journal of Sociology* 77 (January): 660–79.

Uchrowi, Zaim. 2013. Interview, Jakarta. May 14.

Underwood, Doug. 2002. *From Yahweh to Yahoo!: The Religious Roots of the Secular Press*. Urbana, IL: University of Illinois Press.

Utomo, Anif Punto. 2010. *17 Tahun Republika: Melintas zaman* [*Republika*: Across the ages]. Jakarta: Harian Umum Republika.

van Bruinessen, Martin. 2013. "Overview of Muslim Organizations in Indonesia." In *Contemporary Developments in Indonesian Islam: Explaining the "Conservative Turn,"* edited by Martin van Bruinessen, 21–59. Singapore: Institute of Southeast Asian Studies.

———. 2015. "Ghazwul Fikri or Arabization? Indonesian Muslim Responses to Globalization." In *Southeast Asian Muslims in the Era of Globalization*, edited by Ken Miichi and Omar Farouk, 61–85. New York: St. Martin's Press.

Vertovec, Steven, and Robin Cohen, eds. 2002. *Conceiving Cosmopolitanism: Theory, Context, and Practice*. Oxford: Oxford University Press.

Waisbord, Silvio. 2000. *Watchdog Journalism in South America: News, Accountability, and Democracy*. New York: Columbia University Press.

Weaver, Paul. 1994. *News and the Culture of Lying*. New York: Free Press.

Welsh, Bridget. 2015. "The PAS Purge of the Progressives." *Malaysiakini*, June 6. www.malaysiakini.com/news/300911.

Wickham, Carrie. 2013. *The Muslim Brotherhood: Evolution of an Islamist Movement*. Princeton, NJ: Princeton University Press.

Williams, Louise, and Roland Rich. 2000. *Losing Control: Freedom of the Press in Asia* Canberra: Asia Pacific Press.

Yaakop, Rosli. 2014. Interview, Kuala Lumpur. July 4.

Yatim, Abdul Hafiz Mohammad. 2013. Interview, Kuala Lumpur. February 14.

Yegar, Moshe. 1979. *Islam and Islamic Institutions in British Malaya, 1874–1941*. Jerusalem: Magnes Press, Hebrew University.

YonYusuf, Yunan. 2011. Interview, Ciputat. August 24.

Zakaria, Hafiz. 2007. "From Cairo to the Straits Settlements: Modern Salafiyyah Reformist Ideas in Malay Peninsula." *Intellectual Discourse* 15 (2): 125–46.

Zakaria, Hazlan. 2010. Interview, Kuala Lumpur. August 16.

———. 2012. Interview, Kuala Lumpur. June 23.

Zulkifli, Arif. 2009. Interview, Jakarta. May 28.

———. 2011. Interview, Jakarta. January 4.

———. 2015. Interview, Jakarta. July 22.

INDEX

PAS and, 19, 69, 70, 72, 74, 83, 87–88;
    renewal in Islam and, 120–22; *Sabili*
    and, 43; *Tempo* and, 3, 121, 122
Islamism: Indonesia, 25, 26, 28, 34,
    36, 41; Malaysia, 68, 69, 87–88;
    Sabili, 23
Islamization: of state, 32; urban middle
    class, 141–42
Ismail, Rahmat, 34, 39, 45–46
isnad (verifying "the chain of
    transmission"), 13–14, 84, 131–32

Jakarta Charter, 25, 27, 43
Jaringan Islam Liberal (JIL, Liberal
    Islamic Network), 19, 21, 37–38, 55,
    124–29, 147n4
Jawa Pos, 12, 126, 128, 131
JIL (Jaringan Islam Liberal, Liberal
    Islamic Network), 19, 21, 37–38, 55,
    124–29, 147n4
journalism, 3–4, 43, 146n5, 147n3;
    American, 10, 13; Arab, 7–8;
    cosmopolitanism and, 111–16; Islamic,
    3–4; *jurnalisme kenabian*, 135; and
    politics, 7–10, 15–18; prophetic, 135;
    and religion, 4, 12–15; secularism
    and, 5, 7, 19–20; training in, 132–33,
    135–36; values, 10–18, 40, 77, 84–85,
    108, 115, 131–37, 142. *See also* Islamic
    journalism; press freedom
Junaidi, Irfan, 51, 64
Jurnal Nasional, 18
Jurnalistik, 14
justice, 148n4; value of, 16–18, 44, 77, 115,
    116, 137, 142
Justice and Development Party (Adalet
    ve Kalkýnma Partisi, AKP), Turkey,
    48, 74
justification, Islamization and, 141–42

Kahn, Joel S., 99
Kamali, Mohammad Hashim, 7, 13–14,
    115–16

KAMI (Kumpulan Aktivis Media
    Independent), 139
Kandill, Hazem, 144n3
Keller, Anett, 60
Kersten, Carool, 5–6, 117
Khiabany, Gholam, 5, 115
KiniTV, 93
Kolili, H. M., 134
Kompas, 53, 60, 126, 130
Kopal, Indrani, 98
Kovach, Bill, 12, 131
Koya, Abdar Rahman, 81–82
Koya Kutty, 81, 82*fig.*, 83
Kurzman, Charles, 125

Lasswell, Harold, 133
Latif, Subky, 73, 77–79
Lazim, Shuib, 104
Lerner, Daniel, 4
LGBT, 64–65, 128, 145n14
liberal Islam, 9, 30, 38–40, 83, 120, 124–29;
    JIL, 19, 21, 37–38, 55, 124–29, 147n4
Liberal Islam: A Sourcebook (Kurzman), 125
liberalism, 16, 17, 124–29; American,
    118; economic neoliberalism, 125;
    independence without, 136–38; *Sabili*
    vs., 30, 38–39, 141; *sepilis* (secularism,
    liberalism, and pluralism), 38–40,
    126–27, 141, 147n4; *Tempo*, 127, 143n5;
    tolerance without, 5, 112, 127–28, 137.
    See also liberal Islam
Liddle, William, 121, 143–44n1
Liow, Joseph Chinyong, 73
Loebis, Amarzan, 116
Loebis, Mochtar, 141
Loh, Deborah, 100
LPDS (Dr. Soetomo Press Institute), 12,
    40, 42–43
Lubis, Mochtar, 11–12, 43

Madinier, Rémy, 53
Madjid, Nurcholish (Cak Nur), 6, 21, 40,
    54, 114, 117, 120–25, 139–41

CPSIA information can be obtained
at www.ICGtesting.com
Printed in the USA
BVOW08*0716290118

506265BV00003B/5/P